WINNING WITH YOUR VOICE

By Morton Cooper, Ph.D.

FELL PUBLISHERS, INC.
Hollywood, Florida

NOTE: Although some of the names have been changed, all of the case histories are factual.

For information address:
Fell Publishers, Inc.
2131 Hollywood Blvd.
Hollywood, Florida 33020

Library of Congress Catalog Card No.

Published simultaneously in Canada by
Prentice-Hall Canada, Toronto

International Standard Book No. 0-8119-0679-5

2 3 4 5 6 7 8 9 0

ACKNOWLEDGEMENTS

Acknowledgements are more difficult for me to write than entire books. There are numerous people to whom I am indebted, especially the many patients who have encouraged me to write about my voice techniques so that others can benefit, too, and that have allowed their stories to be told. In addition, I am grateful to the celebrity patients who have allowed their names to be mentioned over the years. Their public acknowledgement of voice help has alerted an unknowing public to this field and has encouraged individuals with voice problems to seek assistance.

I must take note here of the individuals from different disciplines who have referred patients to me over the years, especially physicians, psychologists, speech pathologists, teachers of singing, and former patients. Specific colleagues whose assistance, friendship, or guidance has given me the support and faith I needed in order to develop in my field are: Virgil Anderson, Ph.D., Lee Travis, Ph.D., Joel Pressman, M.D., Henry J. Rubin, M.D., Elise Hahn, Ph.D., Benjamin Kagen, M.D., and Gershon Lesser, M.D.

To the American Speech-Language-Hearing Association, for providing an ear and a forum, over the years, to my revolutionary approach to voice training, covering a range of hitherto ignored voice disorders. And to the many thousands of Speech and Language Pathologists and Audiologists who helped provide better speech, hearing and communication through their needed services to the public. I am indebted to them for their many kindnesses and willingness to hear my views. Here's hoping they will use my simple, innovative techniques to help people get better voices or improve troubled voices.

Also, I want to thank specific people for their contribution in bringing this book to life:

Marcia Ann Hartung Cooper, M.A., my wife, also a speech pathologist, for helping me express and define my thoughts of voice training and voice rehabilitation in this book, and in many other books and articles over the past twenty-five years.

The staff at Fell Publishers: Donald Lessne, publisher, for his trust and support in publishing this book; Barbara Newman, speech pathologist, who recommended this book so highly she made the publication possible; Elizabeth Wyatt, editor, for bringing a sharper focus and a clearer perception of what "Winning With Your Voice" is about; and Johanna Porter-Connell, art director, who was able to translate my crude sketches into polished visuals.

Fred Basten, for his literary assistance in organizing reams of my material and his outstanding ability in putting form to it.

Jim Heacock, for his persistence in finding me the right publisher who really believes in "Winning With Your Voice."

Irwin Zucker, for being a mainstay in getting me heard, listened to and read.

Hettie Tack for her secretarial assistance.

Marla and Lorna Cooper, for typing the manuscript on the computer.

I greatly value the assistance or encouragement of each of the above named individuals. I hope finding your Winning Voice gives you as much pleasure as I receive from watching my patients find theirs, and that you go on to a more successful and satisfying life, professionally and socially.

Sincerely,

Morton Cooper, Ph.D.

ABOUT THE AUTHOR

Morton Cooper has been helping people find strong, healthy, natural voices for more than 30 years. Using his voice techniques, countless people have found their natural voice in seconds and, with practice, developed a more effective, winning voice. His Direct Voice Rehabilitation technique has helped hundreds of people suffering from serious voice problems, or recovering from surgery, regain their voice and resume their lives, after they had been told their case was virtually hopeless.

Dr. Cooper developed an interest in the speaking voice when he lost his own voice, after two well-meaning college professors told him to use a deep throat voice to replace his own nasal-sounding voice. As a result, he developed laryngitis, tired voice, throat clearing, and had difficulty being heard, all classic symptoms of the misused voice. After seeing 12 medical physicians that ran him through a gamut of tests and, among other things, told him he was dying of cancer, the 13th doctor actually listened to his voice and understood that the problem was being caused by a misused speaking voice. After a period of months, some of the symptoms were abating and the voice was coming back. At which point Dr. Cooper decided to do his graduate studies specializing in speech and the speaking voice. Based on his own experiences, he decided to help others help themselves, and over several years developed his simple, revolutionary techniques to a "winning voice."

Dr. Cooper is a licensed Speech Pathologist and is certified by the American Speech-Language-Hearing Association (ASHA). He received a certificate of appreciation from ASHA that reads, "in recognition of a significant contribution to the American Speech-Language-Hearing Association and to the profession of speech pathology and audiology." He has been the director of the Voice and Speech Clinic at UCLA Medical Center.

He is a consultant and regular speaker at the Pritikin Longevity Center. He has been an instructor at UCLA teaching voice training and voice therapy. He was involved in training films on voice for the Los Angeles County Schools. He has written regular columns for both a weekly and a monthly publication, as well as chapters in several leading professional speech pathology handbooks.

Dr. Cooper has appeared on numerous television talk shows including: *The Oprah Winfrey Show, Hour Magazine, The Today Show, Good Morning America, CNN, The Merv Griffin Show,* Regis Philbin, and Joe Franklin. On radio, Dr. Cooper has been heard nationally with Larry King, Michael Jackson, Ray Briem, Owen Spann, and many others.

Interviews with Dr. Cooper regarding his techniques have been published in *USA Today, The Los Angeles Times, The Washington Post, US Magazine, Mademoiselle* magazine, *The New York Times Sunday Magazine,* and *The Wall Street Journal.*

He has travelled extensively, speaking at colleges and universities all over the country; he also has been a speaker at numerous medical facilities including Cedars-Sinai Medical Center, UCLA Medical Center, Los Angeles Neurological Society, St. John's Hospital, and Kaiser-Permanente Hospital.

Dr. Cooper received his master's degree from Indiana University and his doctorate degree from the University of California at Los Angeles.

He and his wife Marcia, also a speech pathologist, live outside of Los Angeles. They have two daughters, Marla and Lorna.

His previous book, "Change Your Voice, Change Your Life," is now in its tenth printing.

To contact Dr. Cooper about his techniques, write: Dr. Morton Cooper, 10921 Wilshire Blvd, Suite 401, Los Angeles, CA 90024. Or call (213) 208-6047.

CONTENTS

INTRODUCTION

In today's high-tech world of sound, no other means of communication surpasses the human voice. Yet Dr. Cooper estimates 25 percent of all Americans use a voice too low in their throats and 50 percent use a voice that is too high, nasal and thin, ruining their chances for success. They ignore the warning signals of trouble ahead and go through life unheard and unappreciated.

Here in this invaluable guide, Dr. Morton Cooper reveals his step-by-step plan for success through correct voice technique. Using his basic exercises, it takes only seconds to find your natural, effective voice, then only minutes a day of practice to keep it. He discusses simple, direct ways to control the six major parameters of voice — pitch, tone focus, volume, quality, rate, and breath support — and thereby have a "winning voice."

Over the years, Dr. Cooper's innovative approach to a "winning voice" has been used successfully by men and women of all ages, from all walks of life. These techniques also have been used by such notables as Henry Fonda, Lucille Ball, Richard Crenna, Cheryl Ladd, entrepreneur Norton Simon, singer Stevie Nicks, Diahann Carroll, and Kirk Douglas, among others.

Nearly everyone has a hidden, "star quality" voice that is strong, full, and effective. Most people don't use what they have because they don't realize it's there. From childhood on, they ignore their voices. They grow up with a voice that not only misrepresents then, but detracts from who they really are.

"Winning With Your Voice" will show you how to have a stronger, healthier voice that will be authoritative, outgoing, and more easily understood. It is a book for everyone who has to talk (like it or not), and wants to make a positive impression on others. Discover how to find and develop your "Winning Voice."

WINNING WITH YOUR VOICE

Chapter 1

THE POWER OF A WINNING VOICE

WHEN YOU SAY "HELLO,"
DOES YOUR VOICE SAY "GOODBYE"?

What a powerful force we have in our voices. It is, by far, our most important feature when presenting ourselves to others. A rich, full voice turns frowns into smiles, opens closed doors, wins friends and influences people. It is heard, listened to and liked, and has the power to enhance the quality of a person's life. It can work miracles.

An unpleasant sounding voice can be devastating. It can lead to family arguments or friction in a romance. It can sour business deals and promotions. A troubled or wrong voice can create unintentional stumbling blocks by turning people off.

Every day, ads promote the latest in electronic communications equipment designed to make working easier and our lives more enjoyable. Yet for all the advanced wizardry, nothing can compete with the sound of the human voice. It is, by far, the greatest communicator of all.

A misused voice tells a lot about you, probably more than you care to tell. Have you heard yourself when you are depressed? When you are elated? When you are afraid or nervous? A wrong voice relays many messages, even those that are best kept to yourself. This is discussed in detail in Chapter 4.

When Henry Kissinger talks, there is a sense of doom and gloom, even when his words are optimistic. Do you hear authority? Do you hear self-assurance? I believe he wants us to feel he is in control; but the sound may be too controlled and his voice may not be representing him as best it can.

I hear Erma Bombeck once said, "If you miss the first few words of Henry Kissinger, forget it, folks!" Kissinger's voice may very well make us tune out. It doesn't come alive because he uses it incorrectly, letting it sag in the lower throat. He speaks from "down deep," trudging along as though he is out of breath, and out of energy.

When James Bond talks, through Roger Moore, we listen. Roger Moore speaks low, much like Henry Kissinger, but Moore's voice energizes us. It is hypnotic. It has volume; it carries. It tells us that he is secure, relaxed, friendly, sensuous.

Although Henry Kissinger and Roger Moore both have bass

voices, they have different sounds. And the sound is the important thing. When Moore says "hello," his voice is a greeting. It welcomes us. When Kissinger says "hello," we nod off.

What does your voice say about you?

You probably already know if your voice is too high or too low. If you are not absolutely certain, that is the first thing to find out. *It is important that you move in the right direction.*

Direction is the key to a winning voice. Should you go higher or lower, softer or louder? That's all you need to know to start on the road to success. It is not necessary to spend weeks, months, even years turning a losing voice into a winner. You should find that voice in seconds. After that, it takes only minutes a day to maintain it.

Start by gently humming the first line of a simple tune, such as "Happy Birthday" or "Row, Row, Row Your Boat," keeping your lips closed. These are songs everyone knows, and their uncomplicated melodies will give your real voice a chance to come out.

A good, winning voice should come *naturally*. I stress the word "natural" because that element is essential if you are to find your true, winning voice. No matter how misused your voice is now, it is almost always possible for you to talk in a richer, fuller, more *natural* voice — one that has "star quality."

Hum "Happy Birthday" once more. *Hum*, don't sing. Few people can really sing, but we can all hum.

As you hummed, did you hear what happened to your voice? Did you feel it going down? Or rising? Your voice should move in whichever direction is natural for you.

Try gently humming the melody again as you read on. Can you feel a balanced vibration around your nose and mouth, in the area known as the mask? You should. It is from there that a good voice is projected. The vibration tells you that the voice is placed correctly.

As you move through the pages of the book, you will learn how this simple exercise, and a few others, can give you a better, more effective voice. And it truly is as easy as one, two, three — proper pitch, balanced tone focus and midsection breath support.

A SOUND VOICE MAKES A SOUND IMPRESSION

Personal impression counts for everything. A strong statement, but true. We spend years educating our minds. We learn to dress and eat well. We try to take care of our bodies. We want to look good, not only for ourselves, but for others. We become someone, an individual with a very unique personal identity. We assume an image.

When you meet someone, it is important to make a strong, positive impression. In a face-to-face encounter, your voice is one of the first things the person notices about you. Over the telephone, it is the only thing.

Remember the Lina Lamont character in *Singin' In The Rain*, played by Jean Hagen? Lina was a glamorous movie star, the darling of the silent screen. But when she opened her mouth, everyone laughed. Lina's voice was exaggerated, but the point is not. The voice can work for or against you. It can make you or break you.

It's a fact of life that a poor sound makes a poor impression. No one likes to listen to a blah, wimpy, or whiny voice, or one that drags, cracks and goes haywire. Too many people today do not take the time to really talk. They speak in grunt language, garbling their sentences with words like "I mean" and "you know?"

Mumblers, grunters, and the like have a difficult time making a name for themselves because they are almost impossible to understand. They cannot express thoughts and ideas clearly. They are asked to repeat themselves. Their voices tire quickly. They aren't heard or listened to.

It takes a sound voice to command attention. Anyone who seeks authority has such a voice — executives, lawyers, teachers, actors, men and women in all occupations. The fact is, *everyone* has such a voice at his or her command, but most don't know how to use it.

A voice is like a diamond. If polished, it glows and attracts. But if it isn't polished, it is just another hidden gem.

VOICE LANGUAGE VS. BODY LANGUAGE

Mike Tyson, the heavyweight slugger, is a big bruiser. He speaks in a thin, light voice.

Howie Long, the professional football player, is another giant. He has the light baritone voice of a teenager.

5

Suzanne Pleshette and Brenda Vaccaro are brilliant actresses and beautiful women. Their voices are gruff and unexpected. Like Mike Tyson and Howie Long, their voices do not match their appearances.

Donna is 34 years old. She works in an advertising agency. "Do something about my voice," she pleaded not long ago. "It's not getting me anywhere. I sound like a kid."

Marie has a daughter in junior high school. Whenever she answers the phone she is mistaken for her youngster.

Bert sells printing supplies. His career is suffering, he complains, because of his voice. He has been told that he sounds weak and uncertain.

There are thousands of stories about people who look great but have poor voices. Poor for them, that is, because their voices are too high or too low, too weak or too gruff. A man should not sound wimpy. A man or woman of any age, particularly if he or she is seeking success, should not sound like a child — or the opposite sex.

Beautiful clothes and perfect stature cannot mask a poor voice. Once the mouth opens, the illusion is shattered.

For most people, the problem starts when they are growing up. Their bodies mature but their voices do not. They simply go on speaking as they always have, believing that is the way they were meant to sound. Then comes the realization that their voices are holding them back.

If this scenario sounds familiar, do not despair. There is nothing really wrong with your voice. You just don't know how to use it.

Your voice is waiting to be helped. It has "star quality" capability, but without training, it will continue to deprive you of your real potential.

You may have already discovered your natural, winning voice by humming "Happy Birthday." Before we go on, hum the melody once again.

As you hummed, were you aware of the slight balanced vibration around your nose and mouth, in the mask area? The "buzz" indicates that you are right on target.

Here is another simple exercise that will help you locate your winning voice.

Say "um-hmm" with your lips closed, as if you are casually responding to a friend in conversation. Repeat several times. "Um-hmm ... um-hmm."

Listen to the sound of your "um-hmm" on a tape recorder. (Always keep a recorder handy to monitor your progress while doing the exercises.) If your voice is normally too low, the "um-hmm" will usually bring it up. Your voice should sound *naturally* higher, richer and fuller, even at this early stage. If your voice is normally too high, energizing your voice with "buzz words" and the Cooper Instant Voice Press should make it *naturally* lower, as I explain later.

HOW TO PUT PIZAZZ IN YOUR VOICE

There is an old saying in management, "If you want to get something done, give it to a busy person." Whoever came up with that saying knew what they were talking about. Busy people do accomplish more. Work stimulates them. They seem more interesting, livelier. Energy attracts.

It's the same with voices. A voice without energy is dull. It has dark, heavy tones that puts people to sleep and makes others want to avoid you. A voice that is light and airy will also put people to sleep, because it lacks energy.

Too many people sound older than they are because their voices lack energy, or pizazz. Talk to them by phone and you imagine they are of an older generation. Meet them directly and you discover they are younger than you had envisioned.

The voice is like a camera; it has to be focused to work properly. When a camera is out of focus, the picture is off. When a voice is out of focus, the sound is off. A poorly focused voice can result in nasality, hoarseness, laryngitis, aches and pains in the throat, and difficulty being heard. The voice fades, breaks, or even gives out altogether. A properly focused voice blends resonance or sound from the mouth and the nose to create a dynamic, winning voice.

When the voice is poorly focused, its energy level is sharply curtailed. It is often necessary to push or force the words, which can be fatiguing. When it is properly focused, the voice comes out easily and with energy. Talking should be effortless; it is one of the pleasures of life. But how many people can honestly say that after speaking continuously?

Lack of energy in the voice results in a thin, weak sound. Unfortunately, the vast majority of Americans speak too softly. Of the countless voices I've heard over the years, most lacked life and energy.

I estimate a high percentage of our society is afraid of speaking up and out. We are a land of muted talkers. No one wants to be a loud mouth. And so voices drift up and away—lighter than air, garbled, unheard and unappreciated, or they drop down, becoming muffled and guttural.

Voices that command attention have *Pizazz*, are *O*pen and *Win*ning. I like to think of them as *POW!* voices because they do not go unnoticed. They turn heads, win friends, and influence people.

How do you get a "POW!" voice? Not by turning up the volume. You don't have to force it, it should come naturally if you use your real, *natural* voice.

Hum "Happy Birthday" once again. Humming will almost always focus your voice, raising or lowering it to your natural level. Feel the buzz around your lips and nose? The balanced buzz tells you that your voice is coming out as it should—forward. If you speak from the mask area your voice will no longer sound weak and thin. It will be stronger, clearer, and energized.

Try "um-hum" again. Repeat. At first, you will hear the added power in your voice and think that you are speaking too loudly. Listen to yourself on a tape recorder. What you hear will surprise you. You won't be a loud mouth, but you will have a voice with pizazz. You don't quite understand yet? Read on.

YOU KNOW YOUR BUSINESS — NOW SOUND LIKE IT

Helen's friends call her "lucky." She's bright, young, ambitious, and attractive. She has a responsible, good-paying position with a solid company. She wants to do even better, and she's working hard to make it happen.

Helen has it all, according to her friends. Helen isn't as sure. "I've had people tell me that my voice is my fortune," she said one day. "I've always been a good talker, but lately, I've been having trouble with my voice."

I could understand why. Helen was misusing her voice, speaking from deep in her throat. There was a time, not that many years ago, when women with low, throaty voices were thought to be assertive and seductive. (The movies glamorized the myth by casting actresses with low or husky voices in career women roles.) Today, the sound of such voices can signal voice trouble.

Helen isn't the only young executive to seek help in recent years. Hundreds of men and women have called or written to express their concerns and describe their symptoms. They tell of once strong voices now fading, frequent throat clearing, voices that tire or give out completely, and severe throat and neck pains.

Craig, an attorney, called in to a radio talk show I was doing. "I was in conference with a client today and my voice started giving out," he said. "It has happened before, but not this bad. I'm worried. Without my voice, I am lost in my work."

I asked Craig to hum "Happy Birthday" and he did. Then I asked him to say it, just the way he hummed it. Within seconds his voice sounded clear, richer, and fuller. The raspiness disappeared. So did the panic and much of Craig's concern. He came in for a consultation and is now working on a series of exercises to keep his voice in strong, working condition.

There are high risk voices, just as there are high risk occupations. Teachers have them. So do executives, salesmen, ministers, lawyers, singers — anyone who talks for a living.

When you know your business, sound like you do. Don't let a poor or misused voice come between you and all you've worked so hard to achieve. A strong, confident, well-used voice won't guarantee success, but it is one of the best means of getting you there.

QUESTIONS & ANSWERS

Q: Do people judge a person by his voice?

A: Many people do. Ask them. They make snap judgments about a person simply from what they hear. Voice is thought to *reflect* a person's personality. That isn't always true because the person may not be using his or her voice correctly, not having had any direction. They may, in fact, be reflecting sounds from family and society. The well-used voice has a "feel-good" sound. It builds the speaker's confidence and makes a positive impression on others. A natural, healthy voice can turn lives around.

Q: Can a good voice make you feel better?

A: Definitely. It gives you assurance that you are "someone," that people are listening to you, not tuning you out. Have you ever noticed during a conversation that people may turn away, forget you, or even ignore you? That may be because your voice isn't representing you as best it can. It doesn't get the attention it, and you, deserve. Once you find your natural voice, you may feel better, be more effective, and be listened to.

Q: What do you mean by pitch?

A: The pitch of voice should be a range of notes centering around the natural or optimal pitch level that you use when you speak.

Q: What difference does a voice make to an executive?

A: Not long ago, the president of a blue chip company spoke before a large group of employees. He sounded unenthusiastic and down. "The audience picked up on that," remarked a top company official. "The executive's voice can lead or deny leadership."

During his administration, Ronald Reagan led the country with his style, his manner, and his voice. When Walter Mondale was running for president, he didn't gain too many ears. In my opinion, his voice had a great deal to do with it.

Q: Why is it that primarily performers — actors, singers, public speakers — work on their voices?

A: This is a voice myth. Henry Fonda was losing his voice when he came to me, prior to filming *On Golden Pond*. I've worked with Anne Bancroft, Diahann Carroll, Richard Crenna, Kirk Douglas, Joan Rivers, Cheryl Ladd, Rob Lowe and many other performers whose voices are their fortunes. But you don't have to be a star to sound like one. The majority of the people I see are not entertainers. They are people who need to communicate, at home and at work, in the kitchen or in the classroom, or at the conference table. In today's highly competitive world, the quality of your voice can have a bearing on the quality of your life.

The fact is, whenever you use your voice to communicate with another person you are speaking in public. That makes you "a public speaker." Shouldn't you put your best voice forward?

Q: Isn't it true that nobody really listens to your voice, only what you have to say?

A: This, again, is a voice myth. It is almost impossible to be successful today without an effective voice. Ask a personnel director. Your voice, and how you sound, could very well be the deciding factor in your landing a job. The words you use during an interview may be on target, strong and self-confident, but if they are said in a weak way, you might as well pick up your resume and go home. When trying to make an impression, words are often less important than the way you say them.

Q: My friends tell me that you can talk your way to success. Is that true?

A: People have been doing that for ages, and they will continue to do so for all time. Talking is one of humankind's basic means of communication. He who knows how to talk—and can talk well—can talk his way to success. There is nothing new, or old, about it. It is just a fact of life.

Q: I have strained my voice. My friends told me not to talk louder than a whisper or else I will strain it further. What do you think?

A: That is a common belief but, in fact, is not true. It's easy enough to talk softly, but then you are not yourself, and you are not using your real voice. More often than not, if you continue whispering or talking softly, you wind up with a serious voice disorder. First, you need to have your throat checked by a doctor. Then you need to learn how to speak properly, and with as much volume and ease as you want. It can be done. In fact, people who were once advised as you were, cannot believe that they ever considered such a myth.

Q: Why should I work on my speaking voice? Isn't it the one I was born with?

A: This is another voice myth. We are all creatures of habit. We get into a voice pattern and stay with it, believing that it is our only option. It is not. I can't put a voice in you, but I can show you how to bring out your God-given *natural* voice, one that has star quality. You can have a voice that is richer, fuller, and easier to listen to.

11

Chapter 2

FINDING YOUR WINNING VOICE — IN SECONDS

THE HUMMING OF AMERICA

Humming is as natural as breathing. Many people enjoy humming. Frank Sinatra is said to hum to warm up his voice. The noted poet William Butler Yeats hummed while writing poems. Constantin Stanislavski, the legendary acting coach, talked about how humming could produce the feel for the right voice.

Have you noticed that your voice changes when you hum? Your humming voice is different from your speaking voice. It's richer, fuller, stronger. Humming can bring out your *natural* voice.

Humming often is your vocal "private eye," your built-in radar system to help you locate your true, normal speaking voice. It guides you without special equipment or expense. You have everything you need to make it work .

If you are serious about improving your voice, and yourself, start by humming. There's no easier, more effective way.

Earlier, you began by humming "Happy Birthday." Hum the tune again now.

Did you feel a slight vibration around your nose and lips, in the mask area? As I stated before, talking in the mask is essential to having a stronger, more effective, *winning* voice.

Once again, hum "Happy Birthday."

Feel the "buzz"? This can indicate natural tone focus and pitch for your voice. Now, rather than humming just the melody to "Happy Birthday," hum the words to yourself with your lips closed. Repeat only the first two phrases, alternating humming and saying the words aloud. "Hum-happy-hum-birthday-hum-to-hum-you, hum-happy-hum-birthday-hum-to-hum-you."

Finally, keep the same voice level and just say the words to the first two phrases.

Another simple tune to use to help focus your voice is the first phrase of "Row, Row, Row Your Boat." First hum the phrase. Then put words between each "hum." Finally, say the words aloud, energizing your voice as you speak.

A famous British actor once asked me, "Where should your tongue be when you hum?"

Until then, I hadn't thought about the position of the tongue.

15

"Where do you place yours?" I asked.

"Against the roof of my mouth," he replied.

I tried it his way, and felt the same buzz in the mask that I did when my tongue was flat. But I liked the tongue flat rather than up. Keeping my tongue on the bottom of my mouth seemed to allow the sound to come forward better.

Actually, the placement of the tongue is not that crucial. It is the focused humming that's important. And that is what I stress to new patients or anyone who is interested in a better, more effective voice.

Several times a week, I appear on radio talk shows where I answer questions from callers who are concerned about their voices. Before I offer advice, I often ask a caller to hum "Happy Birthday" or "Row, Row, Row Your Boat." Even over the telephone it is easy to hear the difference between their speaking voices and humming voices. Humming is the most basic of all vocal exercises, and the fastest way to find one's natural voice. That is, the natural, God-given voice.

Once you have found yours, don't stop humming. Hum the words of your newspaper each morning to relax your "morning voice," while raising or lowering the pitch to your natural level. (Johnny Carson, a great talker, has what I call the "morning voice"; he calls it the grumpies.) Hum the words of a book or memo from time to time during the day. Hum the names on street signs as you drive along. Hum the names of products as you scan the shelves in your market. As you think to yourself, hum your thoughts. Hum whenever you can.

Humming can revitalize an older voice and make it sound young again. Humming is a key to unlocking the voice that can lead you to greater success.

UM-HMM: YOUR PUBLIC 'HMMM'

Say "um-hmm," as if you are responding to someone in conversation. Keep your lips together and try not force the sound. Be as spontaneous and sincere as possible.

"Um-hmm."

Again.

"Um-hmm."

Say "um-hmm" once more, then follow with "one."

"Um-hmm ... one."

Could you hear the difference in your voice when you said "um-hmm" and "one"? For most people, there is a noticeable difference. Because while "um-hmm" tends to bring out your new, natural voice, the number was probably spoken in your old voice. Try it again, keeping the "um-hmm" and the number at the same pitch level and tone focus.

Could you feel the sound vibrating around your nose and mouth when you said "um-hmm"? The "buzz" is telling you where your voice should be placed, and the tone you should use. It may also be telling you that the voice you have been using for so long is not really "yours" at all, at least, not the natural voice you believed it to be.

Let's talk about the buzz or vibration. The area around the lips and nose is called the mask. (See **Diagram A**) This term comes from ancient Greek times when male actors literally spoke through a mask when portraying women, since women were not allowed on stage.

To begin with, the throat or pharynx extends from your eyebrows to your voice box, located at the fifth and sixth vertebra of the neck (there are seven vertebra in the neck). It can be divided into three resonance zones, the lower or laryngo-pharynx area (the voice box), the middle or oro-pharynx area (the mouth), and the upper or naso-pharynx area (the nose).

The throat is shaped like a megaphone, the narrow portion beginning at the voice box and widening as it moves upward to the eyebrows. (See **Diagram B**) The basic sound of the voice is produced at the vocal cords. This sound is very light. The amplification of this sound is produced in the mask (around the lips and nose) or as

Diagram A

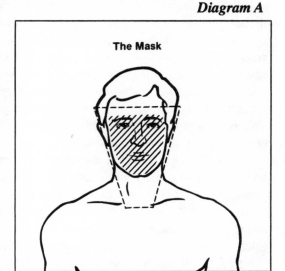

The Mask

17

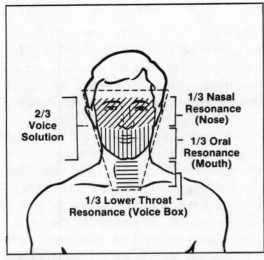

2/3 Voice Solution

1/3 Nasal Resonance (Nose)

1/3 Oral Resonance (Mouth)

1/3 Lower Throat Resonance (Voice Box)

Diagram B

I term it, the two-thirds solution, referring to the upper two resonance areas. All good or great voices are focused in the two-thirds solution area. The blend of oral and nasal resonance is what creates the vibration in the two-thirds mask area and makes an efficient and aesthetic voice.

Nasal resonance is a key element in making the voice alive and well. But, too much nasal resonance makes the voice nasal sounding. **(See Diagram B—tip of nasal area.)** The fear of nasal resonance causes many people to use lower throat resonance. Forced lower throat resonance causes voice problems, including tired voice, hoarseness, lack of carrying power, and other negatives associated with a wrong voice. **(See Diagram B—lower throat area.)**

Mask resonance is not only the key to a winning voice, but also voice health and longevity of voice. It provides carrying power, strength, and durability of tone. It gives you everything you ever wanted in your voice and more. Balanced resonance allows you to project your voice with more or less volume, with ease and comfort. This is the technique good public speakers and talented actors rely on when on stage without a microphone.

Now, let's get back to locating your voice. Like humming, "um-hmm" helps you find your natural voice in seconds. In the past, it was necessary to work with a piano, using musical scales. The problem with that method, aside from needing special equipment, was someone had to go up and down the keyboard with you and identify your natural pitch. The process is complicated, even with an experienced therapist. "Um-hmm" is nature's pitchpipe, and you carry it with you everywhere. Your natural pitch should be at least two or three notes above the bottom of your pitch range.

Once you find your natural voice with "um-hmm," then what? You want to use your voice at that level until you get used to the feel and sound of it; until you can say, "That is me. That is *my* voice."

It will take time for you to become accustomed to your new voice. Before you are ready to use it — really use it — you must feel comfortable with it. A new voice needs "breaking in" just like a new pair of shoes. So stay with "um-hmm" until you can say "um-hmm ... one, um-hmm ... two, um-hmm ... three" and so forth (up to ten) in a natural, easy, and sincere way. Don't force or push the sound. Keep it light and spontaneous, as if you are agreeing with a friend. Again, be sure that the "um-hmm" and the number are at the same pitch level and tone focus.

Practice throughout the day, a few seconds here, a few seconds there. Practice when you are alone or with people. No one will know what you are doing. "Um-hmm" is a perfectly acceptable response in conversation and it is your way of practicing in public.

Your next step is to move from the "um-hmm" to just "hmm," which can be used during your private practice moments. "Hmm" is a basically well-focused and balanced tone incorporating oral and nasal resonance, and gives you the feeling of a natural and focused voice.

Now try "hmm-one," "hmm-two," "hmm-three." If you energize the "hmm," you will get a tingle around the lips and the nose, or mask area. Be sure that the number is at the same pitch level and tone focus as the "hmm."

THE COOPER INSTANT VOICE PRESS

Have you been able to locate your natural pitch by humming or using the "um-hmm" method? Your *natural* pitch is your optimal pitch, and it is most likely different from your *habitual* pitch.

Test yourself once more. Hum the first line of "Happy Birthday." Now say "um-hmm ... one," "um-hmm ... two," "um-hmm ... three."

Did you feel a slight resonance around your nose and mouth as you did the exercises? The tingle tells you that you're placing your voice correctly.

19

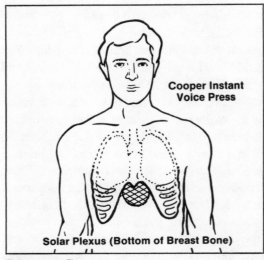

Cooper Instant Voice Press

Solar Plexus (Bottom of Breast Bone)

Diagram C

Perhaps you still are not certain that you have found your natural pitch level and tone focus. An excellent backup exercise is the Cooper Instant Voice Press, which has been so successful that patients often refer to it as "pressing your magic button." (**See diagram C**) The Instant Voice Press is a holistic technique that basically gives you the correct tone focus, natural pitch level and range, and the sound of your real voice. Contrary to prior techniques that worked with only one element at a time, this is a simple 3-for-1 procedure that gives you "everything in a nutshell."

Begin by placing one hand on your solar plexus (the area at the bottom of the breast bone.) Relax your stomach so that it moves in and out as you breathe. With your lips closed, hum while repeatedly pressing your solar plexus with your fingers in a light, quick fashion. "Hmmmm." (Hold that hum.) "Hmmmmmmmmm." Because of the pressing, the "hmm" will actually break up into short bursts of sound like "hmm-hmm-hmm-hmm-hmm ...."

Do this exercise once again. Close your lips and hum while lightly pressing your fingers at the bottom of the breast bone, where the two sides of the rib cage join. As the sound escapes, you will feel a buzz around your mouth and nose. You are actually directing your voice into the mask area, precisely where it should be.

Next, do the Instant Voice Press with your mouth open, saying "Ahhhhh." I have used these techniques for years to help individuals find their real voices in seconds.

Next, try the exercise again, adding a number as you press. This should sound like "hmm-hmm-one," "hmm-hmm-two," "hmm-hmm-three." Then use "ah-ah-one," "ah-ah-two," "ah-ah-three."

Finally, carry this sound over to talking, beginning with one word at a time. "Ah-put-ah-the-ah-milk-ah-out." Keep the sentence short and learn to talk on the buzz.

Can you achieve that same pitch level without pressing your magic button? Raise both hands high above your head and repeat the following words with energy. "Right." "No." "Really." I call these words "buzz words"; they help bring your real voice forward.

Revert to the Instant Voice Press, humming, and buzz words whenever you seem unable to locate your correct pitch level. In fact, it's a good idea to start your day with these exercises.

BUZZING YOUR WAY TO A BETTER VOICE

Buzz words are wonderful. They bring voices forward, to the mask. They lift voices up and out, make them rich and full. They are energy words. Buzz words tell you where your *natural* sound should be. They indicate correct pitch, tone, and focus. They help you develop the voice you need to become a winner.

Buzz words make the area around your nose and mouth tingle, which is a sign of correct voice placement. Don't fight the sensation.

Some buzz words work better than others. I've heard patients argue over which buzz words best bring forth the resonance in the mask. I never take sides. What works for one person may not help another. So it is up to each individual to determine the most effective words to use.

Which buzz word works best for you? Is it "right"? Is it "really?" Is it "no"?

Here are others to try:

Hello	Do	Hey	Wow	Oh	Might
Ready	Great	Go	Show	Push	Be

Alternate these words from time to time as you perform the following exercises. While each of them helps to naturally bring your voice forward, to the mask, remember to speak them as if you *really* mean them. In other words, when you say "right," say it with conviction. *Right*!

Stand straight, with your hands stretched over your head.
Say "Oh!"

"Right!"

"Really!"

"Um-hmm."

Now, still standing, bend forward from the waist as far as you can. Let your head and arms dangle loosely. Then say buzz words followed by numbers. Keep in mind that the number should be at the same pitch level and tone focus as the buzz word.

Say "really!"

"Really ... one!"

"Really ... two!"

"Really ... three!"

"Really ... four!"

"Um-hmm."

Next, stand straight again. With your arms at your sides, say "right!"

Say "hello!"

"Really!"

"Ready!"

"Ready!"

"Um-hmm."

"Um-hmm"

Relax.

As you performed the exercises, were you conscious of the resonance about your nose and mouth? With the "buzz" your voice should have taken on a new richness, clarity, and efficiency. It should have found its *natural sound.*

Are you ready to go one step farther? Stand with your arms at your sides and repeat the last exercise.

Say "RIght!"

"Hello!"

"Really!"

"Um-hmm."

"Um-hmm-*my*-um-hmm-*name*-um-hmm-*is*-um-hmm-(*your name*)."

Did you feel the buzz? Did you hear your natural voice, the voice you can use all day without fatigue or hoarseness? If you didn't tape record yourself during the exercise, do it now, then listen to the playback. If your voice was too high, it should have come down. If too low, it should have risen. The change may only be subtle, but you will notice a difference — a positive difference. You can have a dynamic new sound that can lead to winning ways. You may find you are heard, listened to, liked, desired by the opposite sex, and can land that job you've been seeking.

With a little practice, your dynamic new, winning sound can become habitually yours.

THE VOICE MIRROR MACHINE

Patients will occasionally tell me that they have trouble practicing. The exercises are simple enough, they say, but "other factors" seem to inhibit them. Some people admit feeling uncomfortable practicing at home because of distractions. Others simply are unsure of themselves. They have hummed, "um-hmmed," tried the Cooper Instant Voice Press and said the buzz words. They hear a new sound, but they cannot believe that it is really theirs. Making the transition from their old, habitual voice to their natural pitch level and balanced tone focus becomes an unsettling experience.

A talk show hostess came to my office not long ago. Her voice was failing and she didn't know why. She had seen a medical doctor, who prescribed medication and rest, but her condition was worsening. She feared her career was in jeopardy.

The young lady talked for a living. As a popular Hollywood resident, she was frequently seen on the town, attending various business functions and social gatherings. Occasionally, she hosted nightlong telethons and, whenever possible, she rooted for her favorite sports team. She was constantly using her voice, often forcing it to be heard above the crowd.

Talking continually is fine. Talking *wrong* continually is not.

With the failure of her voice came emotional stress and strain. She let her feelings dictate her pitch level. She spoke low and from down in the throat.

"Your voice will come back once you get it out of your lower throat," I told her. "It is essential you keep your pitch *up*." She hummed for me, then practiced the buzz words. She could feel the tingle around her nose and mouth, and hear the difference in her voice. It sounded normal, natural, and healthy.

She was thrilled to have her proper voice back again, and so easily. But now she was concerned she might lose it as quickly as she had found it.

"Not as long as you talk at the same pitch level where you hum," I said. "Let your hum be your guide. Go under it and you'll wind up in the lower throat, your danger zone. The key is to speak in the tone of your hum, or 'um-hmm,' then carry the tone focus into conversation."

"And how do I do that?" she asked.

"By practicing."

She was back in the office a few days later. "I can't do it at home," she said. "I can't even exercise at home. I have to go to a gym."

I led her into a practice room and sat her before a small device often used for office therapy, called a Voice Mirror Machine. About the size of a 19 inch monitor, two columns of lights marked with the corresponding musical notes blink on and off in response to the patient's speaking or humming. By showing the patient's pitch level in lights, this instrument provides immediate visual feedback for proper voice placement. (I direct the patient to the correct pitch level and contrast it with the old pitch level.)

I asked her to hum "Happy Birthday" and watch as the lights flickered on the screen. "Now I can *hear and see* where my voice should be placed," she said. The lights made practicing easier for her.

I cautioned her, then, against relying too heavily on the Voice Mirror Machine. Soon she would have to learn to place her voice correctly on her own, since she wouldn't always have the device. "Check the lights to make sure you stay within your natural range," I told her. "At the same time, be conscious of the buzz around your nose and lips. Always go for the buzz."

In a different atmosphere, working with the machine, the talk show hostess was suddenly able to practice. She hummed "Happy Birthday" again, and said the buzz words. She then began the following series of voice exercises created specifically for people who talk too low in pitch.

These exercises can be used anywhere. But, they are recommended *only* if your voice is focused in your lower throat, not if you have a sound that is too high or nasal. If you are talking from the lower throat, and your hum indicates that your pitch should be raised, include these exercises in your daily practice routine.

24

Start by saying "zim-zim."

Repeat. "Zim-zim."

Do you feel the buzz in the mask area, that is, around your nose and mouth? The buzz is nature's guiding light. It tells you when you have the correct tone and focus. Make sure you feel the buzz before you proceed.

Repeat "zim-zim." Then "zim-zim ... one, zim-zim ... two, zim-zim ... three" on up to ten, maintaining the same pitch and focus.

The following is what I call the Cooper Vowel Chart. It is a unique system that can help you correctly place your voice is the mask area, around the nose and lips. Locate your correct vowel group and begin the exercise.

COOPER VOWEL CHART

The vowels listed under Group I are for voices that are too low, too far down in the throat. Those in Group II and Group III should be used only if your voice is too high and thin. With each vowel, count from one to ten, remembering to keep the same pitch and tone focus on the numbers as you use on the vowels. Put energy in your voice as you practice.

Group 1	Group 2	Group 3
Me-Me	Mo-Mo	Mu-Mu
Ne-Ne	No-No	Nu-Nu
Ze-Ze	Zo-Zo	Zu-Zu
Zim-Zim	Za-Za	Ma-Ma

GETTING INTO THE RIGHT VOICE

Before you try conversation, test your new voice at home with the following sentences. They contain non-emotional, non-threatening words to bring your new voice forward. Feel for the all-important buzz around your lips and nose as you speak. (Practice the first few sentences until you feel comfortable with them, then practice a few more. Repeat before moving on.)

As you proceed with the practice sentences, monitor yourself before each one with a casual and sincere "um-hmm," which can help you readily re-establish proper pitch level and tone focus. "Um-hmm" whenever you feel it is necessary. Keep in mind that it can be between sentences or between words within the sentences.

Say, "um-hmm." Feel the buzz, then continue to talk at that level.

These sentences can be helpful if you are too high in pitch:
1. The law saw him withdraw from fiction to reality.
2. He drew a claw with a hacksaw and it was without a flaw.
3. A mall is not a hall, but a hall may become a mall.
4. A man with a horn is like a writer who has found his form.
5. He had corn in the morning, and prawns for lunch, and at evening he crawled and sprawled on the lawn while he talked about the raucous bunch.
6. She was enthralled by the shawl he bought for her stall, until she found it was neither too tall nor too small.
7. What one ought often do, one almost always seldom does.
8. We are all always ready for awful awesome events, but seldom prepared for simple awkward situations.
9. Words such as "all, always, also, almost, already, often, awful" and such are almost always too all inclusive in meaning.
10. All is not what it appears to be because we often ought disguise the core of the matter.

These sentences can be helpful if you are too low in pitch:
1. The bright light had a light that could shine through the night.
2. The butterfly asked why while quite on high, and in the rain was still quite dry, as it did fly and went bye-bye.
3. Be you, be me, whomever you be, be happy.
4. He said that three and three must equal be.
5. The peak seemed to lean toward the deep reach of leaves.
6. He who eats as a treat may find himself heavy upon his feet.
7. Dream and you dream alone; scream and you scream alone; lean upon a team and you are better for that scheme.
8. The soil was a foil like his voice was a coil.
9. The mouse was in town down in the ground building his house.
10. He had a gray sleigh that was sprayed with clay as he played.

GETTING INTO CONVERSATION

Through repetition of the voice exercises and practice sentences, you've familiarized yourself with various ways to locate your correct pitch and tone focus. You may even have tested your new sound in conversations with friends by sprinkling your responses with spontaneous and sincere "um-hmms" or buzz words.

It's possible, and quite understandable, that you may be hesitant to say more than "um-hmm" during this period of discovery. You wonder how your friends will react to your new voice. You're not quite sure of it yourself. Does it sound phony?

That's a natural concern. After all, you've been speaking in your old voice for many years. Getting away from it may be a little difficult, but no more so than breaking any bad habit.

How do you make the transition to using your dynamic new voice in conversation? You ease into it slowly, starting with an "um-hmm" response and following with an occasional buzz word, such as "right "or "really," whichever seems appropriate. Let the buzz words be your guide. They will help you carry your natural pitch and tone focus into conversation.

Should you feel yourself slipping back into your old, habitual voice, stop momentarily and "um-hmm." The slight pause as you talk will be barely noticeable, and it will get you back on the right track. And your frequent "um-hmms" as you respond to the other person should keep you there. This technique will be helpful as you use your new voice in conversation.

PRACTICE MAKES IT HAPPEN

You can find your natural voice in seconds, but it takes practice to keep it.

Practice is not something you *have* to do; you do it because you want to improve your voice. Only by practicing can you learn to identify, locate, and establish the right voice, the one you want to represent you.

"Um-hmm ... one." "Um-hmm ... two." "Um-hmm ... three." "Hmm-one." "Hmm-two." "Hmm-three."

Contrary to popular opinion, practice does not always make perfect. Wrong practice leads to wrong results or what is known as "permanent wrong." Right practice, however, makes "permanent right."

How do you know if you are practicing correctly? Let the buzz words, the "um-hmm," or the Instant Voice Press be your guide.

When you do the exercises, do you feel a slight resonance or tingle around your nose and lips? You should if you are doing the exercises right.

Don't try to force or push the buzz. You'll only create an unnatural resonance. What you want is an easy, *natural* resonance, with a soft ring or buzz to it. You can feel the buzz slightly when you exercise correctly.

Place the finger of one hand on the bridge of your nose and the other hand lightly over your lips. Now hum "Happy Birthday" or "Row, Row, Row Your Boat." A soft resonance should be barely discernible.

Next, take one hand and place it lightly over your Adam's apple. Hum the tune again. Do you feel a slight vibration there, as well as around your nose and mouth? The buzz should not be stronger in any one area, but should be evenly distributed.

As I mentioned earlier, to make sure you are getting the right sound in your voice, you should practice as much as possible throughout the day. Constant repetition of the exercises is part of your retraining, as it reinforces the proper pitch level and tone focus. In other words, the more you practice, the faster your new voice will become natural to you, if you are practicing correctly.

Start by practicing 5 minutes a day. You needn't practice all five minutes at one time — 30 seconds here, 30 seconds there will suffice, as long as you practice each hour. Later, as you become more voice-conscious and tuned into your proper voice level, you can eliminate some practice time. By then, however, you should be using your new voice in public.

Practicing in public should help speed your improvement. You can easily practice while among others by responding spontaneously with "um-hmm," since it is an acceptable response in conversation. When alone, remember you can focus your voice with a simple "hmm" in the mask, spoken in a brief rat-a-tat manner.

Although the exercises are simple, you may find it difficult to stay with a regular practice routine, especially at the start. It might be helpful for you to work with a friend or colleague from time to time. You will, of course, have your tape recorder handy (always consider that as an invaluable partner), but you may feel the need for direct encouragement and reinforcement in order to reach your goal. A family member or a close friend can provide emotional support, if necessary, while helping to monitor your progress.

Are you maintaining your correct voice level? Are you moving too quickly or too slowly, accomplishing as much as you'd like or too little? Is your humming spontaneous or forced? Having someone around to answer your questions and offer suggestions often makes practicing easier. It's also nice to be able to share a feeling of accomplishment as your voice becomes richer, fuller, and stronger.

If you still have difficulty finding your new voice, I would suggest you seek help from a professional voice therapist, preferably one trained in the Cooper voice method. But, if you have continued hoarseness or any persistent voice problem, see a physician. Be aware that serious voice problems (growths, spastic dysphonia, paralyzed vocal cord, etc.) also require professional help.

Practicing your new voice is up to you. It's not enough to simply run through the exercises each day. You must follow the simple guidelines and practice correctly. Only right practice makes "permanent right."

"Um-hmm ... one." "Um-hmm ... two." "Um-hmm ... three."
"Hmm-one." "Hmm-two." "Hmm-three." "Um-hmm ... *right*."
Right!

QUESTIONS & ANSWERS

Q: Is it possible to have permanent laryngitis?

A: Some people think they do, and they think it is the way things have to be. But that's not necessarily true because permanent laryngitis doesn't exist ordinarily. If laryngitis or hoarseness lasts more than two weeks, the individual should see a medical doctor. So-called "permanent laryngitis" without medical cause merely indicates that you are hurting your voice by using it as you do. Nearly all the cases of "laryngitis" I have seen are not permanent at all. They are temporary, due to voice misuse and abuse. But continued wrong use of the voice creates a voice that leaves both patient and listener believing nothing can be done.

Q: I have been told to rest my voice, but I have to talk. What do I do?

A: You can talk all day long, under normal circumstances, if done correctly; your voice should go on and on, clearly and easily. There are exceptions, however. If you had surgery, you should rest your voice briefly—not long. If you yelled at a game and went hoarse, you should rest your voice. But if you are misusing your voice, resting it won't help. Once you start talking again, your voice will tire and continue to bother you. You need to learn how to use your voice properly.

Q: Talking is a major part of my job. I love to talk, but my voice tires easily. Is there something wrong with me? Some people can talk forever.

A: You don't know how to speak properly. You are using the wrong voice, either talking in the lower throat or too high in the throat. You must learn to balance the tone.

Q: My voice seems to get better as I lose weight. Is there any connection between the two?

A: The voice *may* be affected by being overweight. The body may tire, and anything that fatigues the body can affect the voice. Generally, the pitch becomes lower. It is much easier to speak lower as you become fatigued by the excess weight. Breathing becomes harder, so you work harder for breath support—and at the wrong pitch. Though being overweight can induce a voice problem, or add to it, the weight need not cause or contribute to voice difficulty. It depends upon the individual, the circumstances, and how the voice is used. Weight is but one factor that affects the voice.

Q: I have been told that my posture is the reason I have a bad voice. Is there any truth to that?

A: Posture has very little to do with voice production. The way you move your head, stand, or sit, is of little importance in the correct use of your voice. If you have a bad voice, it is due to incorrect pitch, tone focus, volume, quality, and breathing.

Q: My voice seems to worsen with a change in the weather. What is the connection?

A: Your emotions, most likely. If you are depressed or morose, the pitch and tone of voice may drop. If you are happy, the voice may rise. However, some people suffering from allergies are indeed affected by the weather. The voice mechanism may react to the pollens and become contained or falter. It needn't.

Q: My voice is always tender. I mean, it isn't very loud and it isn't heard very easily. It has always been that way. Is this natural and normal?

A: The tender voice is neither natural nor normal. It simply indicates that you are using your voice improperly. The natural voice has life, volume, and range. The abnormal voice has what you call a "tender" sound and feeling. The answer is to learn to use your voice naturally.

Q: I'm a 19-year-old guy with two voices. I have a very high voice, and a low voice. When I speak I never know which voice will pop out. What is happening to me? Can I do anything about it? It isn't very funny anymore.

A: You are between your old and new voices. Puberty and the change in body and mental structure have played havoc with your voice. Your high-pitched, falsetto voice is your old, established voice. The new, low-pitched voice is more your natural voice. It is essential you learn how to control the new voice, which pops into your speech now and then, and interrupts the high, falsetto voice you are still using. You are ready and able to use the new voice. Try it. Pitch your voice down, and let it stay low for a few weeks. The exercises in this book will help you.

Q: Why don't I have a loud voice anymore? I try to shout but no one hears me.

A: You did a little too much talking, in the wrong way. After you have abused your voice, your ability to make it louder is noticeably diminished. You might be arriving at a point where your vocal muscles have about taken all the punishment they can endure. The voice shows it's in trouble by its inability to be loud, or have any kind of normal or acceptable type of volume.

Q: I know I have misused my voice for years. If I get my natural voice, will it stay with me?

A: If you learn how to use your voice well, it should get stronger, bigger, and better. Keep this in mind. Of a 1974 follow-up study involving 128 of my voice patients, 98% were rated excellent or good from three months to seven years after completing voice therapy.

Chapter 3

THE GREAT AMERICAN VOICE DIET

GETTING INTO VOICE TRAINING

In business, we are virtually nameless without a "calling card" to announce who and what we are. Your voice is also a "calling card." Don't you want it to represent you at your best?

It isn't enough to have a voice that simply transmits words. To make a name for yourself and improve your position in life, your voice should be distinctive, full, rich, and dynamic. It has to sound good to be heard, listened to, and liked. A good, winning sound transmits how you feel about yourself.

Most people have incredible voices — voices that are wonderfully appealing. But they don't use them because they don't know they have them.

Kevin has an incredible voice, but it took him some time to realize it. A struggling computer salesman, Kevin spent his mornings making calls and his afternoons at the local gym playing basketball. Nearing 30, he had an unpleasant sounding voice, whiny and nasal. "I've talked that way since I was born," he said one day. "Impossible," I told him. "No one is born with a voice like that."

Kevin first heard his natural voice at the gym. When another player fouled him, or he got upset, he let out a bellow. Suddenly, his voice was no longer whiny, but booming. The sound of Kevin's natural voice caught the other players by surprise. They stopped to listen, and he began to earn their respect. Now Kevin uses what he calls his "basketball voice" and he is earning more than respect, his income has doubled.

Successful people who use their voices for a living, even those in the public eye, were not born with the voices you hear. They were born with the ability to have good and great voices. They *learned* to use them. We all have the *ability*. It is God-given and natural. But you need direction, and a sense of how to make your voice work for you.

How do you know when it is time to get into voice training? Ask yourself these questions: Do I honestly like my voice? Do I become self-conscious when I hear the sound of my voice? Does my voice create a positive image for me? Does my voice tire or give out easily? Do people ask me to repeat myself? Is my voice holding me back?

Perhaps a good friend has remarked about your voice. A *good* friend is more likely to comment, wanting to be helpful. Business associates and social acquaintances rarely bother. You are simply left to wonder about missed opportunities.

If you honestly don't know, listen to yourself on a tape recorder. Do you like what you hear? Is it a voice that sounds warm, dynamic, inviting? Does it exude confidence? Is it a voice you would hire—a voice that makes you want to listen?

If your voice doesn't have a winning sound, don't despair. Such a voice can be yours, and sooner than you may realize.

THE TIME FACTOR

One of the first questions new patients ask is, "How long will it take to improve my voice?" I know what they want to hear, a sincere promise of "one or two lessons," even "overnight."

It seems that everyone is in a hurry these days. We've become accustomed to living in a world of instant coffee, fast food, and fast-forward movies. We're always on the lookout for quick and easy ways to get things done.

The truth is, it takes only *seconds* to find a better, more dynamic voice, and then only *minutes* a day to maintain it. It is easy to find your winning voice, but to make it habitual—that is, to speak naturally and spontaneously in your new voice—will take some work.

How long did it take you to learn to drive a car? Some people become expert after only a few lessons. Others take a few months, maybe longer.

How long does it take to travel from one side of the country to the other? Doesn't it depend on how you do it? If you fly in a jet, it takes only hours. If you go by bus, it takes days. In a car, making frequent stops, it can take a week or more. The time you spend getting there is entirely up to you.

It's the same with retraining the voice. You can do it quickly or slowly, it is your choice. Success, however, will depend on how carefully you follow the easy exercises outlined. Cooperation and determination are the real keys. You must be willing to break old habits and change your voice image. You must *want* to improve your voice, and enhance your career or social relationships.

The average person makes the transition in three to six months.

With some people, a new, natural voice becomes automatic in one to three months. Some do it almost overnight. Most often, you are the key. (Patients with serious voice problems require longer periods of therapy.)

It's not realistic to set a time limitation for yourself since everyone progresses at a different rate. Just know that once you find your winning voice — and it can come almost instantaneously — it is yours to keep. But not without work, and a willingness to succeed.

THE SOUND OF YOUR NEW VOICE: THE VOICE IMAGE

Be prepared not to like your new voice at first. If you are like most people, it will sound and feel unnatural. But don't be discouraged. Stay with it, and soon it should begin to feel both natural and normal.

A major factor in changing from a wrong voice to a right voice is your voice image. The voice image is the way you hear yourself. It is the key psychological and emotional element as you find and use your new natural voice. Your old voice is part of you, and you hàve become so accustomed to it that any alteration may make you uncomfortable. The new voice may sound too loud, too full, too rich, and too different. If you ask others about your new voice, it is extremely credible and believable. You must discard your old voice image and establish and accept a new one based on your new, natural voice.

Annie, a high school teacher from the Midwest, is a typical case in point. For years, she spoke softly. Her voice was dull, monotonous, without conviction and authority. It turned her students off, she said. No one paid attention to her.

Annie's new voice was well-modulated and strong, radiating self-confidence. She wasn't happy with it either. "It's not me," she remarked. "It doesn't *sound* like me."

"Is that why you don't like it?" I asked. "Or is it because you're not used to it?"

"Both," she answered quickly. Then, with some hesitation, she added, "I'm not quite sure. It's just ... so different."

Annie's voice *was* new and different. "You will have to use it for awhile before it feels normal to you," I told her.

"I don't think I can use it," she said. "It sounds strange. My students will laugh at me."

I asked Annie to make a recording of her new voice; then we played it back. "Tell me about your new voice now," I said.

Her face brightened. "It's really not as bad as I thought," she said. "To be honest, it's actually quite pleasant."

"Then you *do* like it?"

"Yes, I do. I really do. It's stronger, more outgoing and commanding."

"But it's not right for you?"

"It *is* right for me, except ...."

"Except what?"

"It sounds like somebody else."

"Who?"

"No one in particular. I'd just never know it was me."

I had to remind Annie about the purpose of her visit. "I thought you wanted to get away from your old sound."

"I did. I do."

"Then give yourself time. It won't be long before you will identify with your new voice." Everyone else would too, I told her, because her new voice — her natural, winning voice — revealed the *real* Annie, a woman people would like, listen to, and respect.

GETTING THE FEEL OF IT

It often takes me only a few seconds to discover what is wrong with a voice. Helping a person change takes longer.

Frank's old voice was gruff and throaty. After raising his pitch, his new voice came out clear and easy.

"It feels flaky," was his first comment. "I sound like a girl." To Frank, after hearing his gravelly voice for so many years, it probably did. To everyone else, it definitely did not.

Frank was so discouraged after hearing his new voice that he nearly gave up. But he was absolutely determined to improve his voice and put an end to the nagging throat clearing that plagued him. "At first, speaking in my new voice wasn't easy," he admitted. "The hardest part was to use it without thinking." Now, he can. "Using the new pitch is like being reborn," he said recently. And his throat clearing has all but disappeared.

Ken found his new voice, then complained that he was going hoarse. "My old voice didn't make me hoarse," he said.

"You sound clear to me," I told him. He *was* clear.

"Well, it's hoarse," he countered. "It *feels* hoarse. I seem to have less power than before." To Ken, less power was equivalent to going hoarse.

I explained what was happening with his voice. Before, he was talking from the lower throat, pushing his voice out. Now, he talked from a different area, the mask. He didn't need to push his voice; it flowed easily and naturally. He would experience some discomfort for a time, caused by increased use of the muscles under the jaw and in the soft palate. But those symptoms would disappear with the consistent use of his proper and natural voice.

Unaccustomed to his new voice placement, Ken insisted, "I still feel hoarse."

I urged him to keep practicing, and he did. A few sessions later, he told me, "I really like the sound of my new voice. And, you know, it doesn't feel hoarse anymore."

I wasn't surprised.

Voices are like old shoes, comfortable and easy to slip into — even if they are not right for us, or cause problems, or hold us back. Your habitual voice has become such a part of you that subconsciously you may not want to part with it. And so you make up excuses, *anything* to delay the change.

Be patient with your new voice. *It is not your old voice.* Give yourself time and it will sound and feel natural to you. It should work for you, and pay big dividends. You can be the "someone" you've always wanted to be. People may begin to respect and admire you, wondering what it is about you that makes them want to be with you. You can radiate energy and confidence. You can sound more dynamic. Now, talking can be fun and exciting. Best of all, you can be the person you've always wanted to be.

PROMISE NOT TO BREATHE A WORD

There is one other factor, however, that you must master before the transition from your old, habitual voice to your new, natural voice can be successfully completed, and that is breathing properly.

You say you already know how to breathe? You simply draw in air and let it out. Right? Well, that's the basic idea. But what about your voice? Does your voice get enough air to support it? There is only one way to find out for certain. Try this easy test.

Sit up straight and hum "Happy Birthday" in an easy, casual way. "Hmm-hmm-hmm-hmm-hmm-hmm .... "

Were you aware of your breathing as you hummed? Not really? Then try one more exercise. Say "um-hmm" and count to five, preceding each number with an "um-hmm."

"Um-hmm ... one."

"Um-hmm ... two."

"Um-hmm ... three."

Were you more aware of your breathing this time? Did your shoulders move up and down as you performed the exercise? Did your chest expand as you breathed in, and deflate as you spoke? If you noticed those things happening, you're like most everyone else.

"Chest out, stomach in!" Where have you heard *that* before? From your parents? From a gym teacher? From an army sergeant? A heaving chest was supposed to exercise the chest muscles and get more air into the lungs, which, in turn, made the blood richer and better. As a child, I was constantly reminded to stand straight with my chest out and stomach in. That was the secret to good posture, everyone told me. Almost all my female patients have told me their mothers instructed them to hold their stomachs in when they breathed. So all of these woman were using upper chest breathing, and it is the same for the men. You can have good posture and breathe correctly, without your stomach protruding. Good breathing is invisible to the eye.

The average person breathes eight to twelve times per minute, more if under stress. The chest cavity is heavy; it takes considerable effort to lift it up and out. Expanding the chest with every breath is not only pointless, it's exhausting.

Have you ever watched a sleeping person or animal breathe? Pets and people at rest breathe as nature intended, from the midsection. So, forget everything you've ever learned about chest breathing, and start breathing as nature intended.

When you use your midsection, or belly muscles, you relieve tension in the small, fragile muscles of the throat, allowing your voice to project

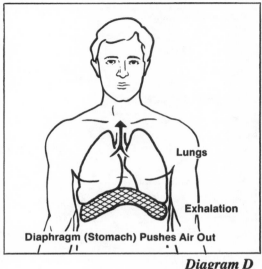

Diagram D

more easily. Your stomach pumps the air up through your mouth and nose. (**See Diagram D**) The air reinforces the voice to make it richer, fuller, more resonant and durable. Without air, we cannot talk.

People who have voice problems, especially severe voice problems such as spastic dysphonia or the "strangled voice" (see Chapter 9), reverse the breathing process by letting the air out before they talk or as they start to talk. Then they are actually speaking without air or with only a minimal amount of reserve air. You can't drive a car on empty. Nor can you speak on empty, without air.

Almost every vocal coach and voice therapist knows you must use midsection breath support. Ask anyone who sings, acts, or uses the voice for a living. Many professionals in these fields will admit they have had voice problems at one time or another caused by improper breathing techniques. The voice demands air. Without enough air, you exhaust your body and foster a voice extremely limited in flexibility and listener appeal.

Breathing from the midsection may be somewhat bothersome at first and, admittedly, a little tiring. But the muscles of the stomach adapt quickly, and once you learn to use them as nature intended, you'll find that you not only have more control of your voice, you'll feel better, too. In addition, using your stomach muscles can trim

41

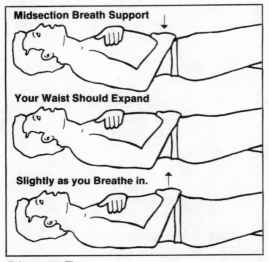

Midsection Breath Support

Your Waist Should Expand

Slightly as you Breathe in.

Diagram E

inches off your waist.

First you need to learn to breathe from your midsection. Sit on a chair with one hand on your chest and the other on your midsection. Breathe easily through your nostrils. Don't force the breathing or take a deep breath. You will find that your midsection moves out as you breathe in and that your chest remains stationary. If your chest is moving up as you breathe, you are breathing wrong for speech.

Another way of learning to breathe for speech is to lie flat on your back, nothing under your head, with one hand on your chest and one hand on your midsection. Relax and breathe in as though you are lying on the beach or in bed getting ready to go to sleep. Your midsection should move up, and the bottom of your waist should expand slightly. Your chest should not move. Practice breathing this way until you become accustomed to the midsection as you breathe through your nostrils. **(See Diagram E)** When you are comfortable with midsection breathing, breathe in through your nostrils, but on exhalation, purse your lips and blow out a steady stream of air. You will feel the midsection move in gradually, smoothly, and progressively as you exhale the air. The next step is to breathe in with your mouth slightly ajar. Exhale through the mouth. Be sure that as you inhale, the chest does not raise. You will notice that your intake of air is faster than your exhalation. Inhalation takes only a fraction of a second, while exhalation may cover a period of 3 to 10 seconds.

When you have gained control of inhalation and exhalation in the reclining position, follow the same procedure in a sitting position. Finally, practice in a standing position.

Now, breathe again. Now exhale slowly. Take another breath. As you let out the air, say "oh" or "ah." Feel the added energy air brings to your voice. The "um-hmm" and the "hmm" also help you breathe correctly, from the midsection.

Everyone breathes at a different rate, but I like to take a breath every four or five seconds so there's enough air to support my voice when I speak. But I vary my breath intake as I talk, depending on the situation.

Once more, breathe from your midsection. Be sure to keep the stomach muscles relaxed. You can't breathe properly holding your stomach tightly in. The troubled voices around us prove that. America is a land of chest breathers, and poor voices. That fact is more than coincidental.

After you have learned midsection breath support, you must coordinate this with the correct pitch level and tone focus. Practice all the exercises from Chapter 2, using midsection breath support.

HEARING THE CHANGES IN YOUR VOICE

Remember the first time you heard your voice played back on a tape recorder? You probably thought, "That's not my voice!" or "I don't really sound like that ... do I?" Chances are you still feel that way whenever you hear yourself. You might even squirm a little.

If you had a difficult time listening to your wrong voice, wait until you hear your right one. Initially, it will sound totally alien to you. Artificial, louder than usual, unreal. You will swear it is *not you*.

There is a reason for that. When you speak, the bones in your head get in the way, forming a barrier of sorts. Your voice must pass through these obstacles before it reaches your ears.

You are too close to your voice to really hear it. You are actually hearing it from the *inside*. It is different from your *outer* voice, the one other people hear when you speak.

Conversely, some patients find it hard to hear changes in their voices. They are too wrapped up in events taking place in their busy lives. Or, they tune in for a moment or two, then get distracted. Before long, they have grown accustomed to their new, natural sound. For them, it has become normal.

Tobi did not recognize a change in her voice. A young professional, and a perfectionist, she began to question why she kept coming to see me, and what she was getting for her time and money. After listening to a playback of her "before" and "after" voices, she commented, "It's unbelievable. I'm really shocked to hear the difference between the two. I had no idea, the change has been so gradual."

Tobi needed to hear herself as others do. She stopped fighting and willingly continued her sessions to perfect subtle changes in her sound. "It works," she said, with new confidence. The young lady likes things that work.

If you are serious about upgrading your voice, it is important for you to hear yourself as others do. That's why I strongly recommend you use a recording device when you practice the voice exercises, whether you are humming, using buzz words, the Cooper Instant Voice Press, or any of the other exercises. By taping your new voice, you should gain a truer sense of how you really sound, not how you *think* you sound. We hear ourselves through bone conduction, which is 3/1,000th of a second faster than air conduction. The bones in our head distort sound. The tape recorder plays back what we actually sound like — and as others hear us — via air conduction.

Always keep a recorder handy. It will not only allow you to monitor your progress, it will help your voice retraining. The tapes help you honestly appraise the changes in your voice.

Hearing yourself will also dispel the sensation of loudness that you will surely experience with your new voice. You will discover that you are not shouting, or speaking any louder than you did in the past. It will simply sound that way to you because your voice has been correctly refocused, to the mask area.

Once again, the sound you are hearing is all in your head. In time, and with practice, you should become comfortable with your new voice and develop a new voice image to go with it; a very positive reflection of yourself.

QUESTIONS & ANSWERS

Q: Once my new voice becomes habitual, will I be able to use my old wrong voice?

A: Your new voice should become so effective that you won't want to speak in your old voice. But if you really want your old voice back, just forget all you've learned about good voice production.

Q: Do you really have to stop and breathe when speaking correctly?

A: Yes, you do — but only temporarily, so no one notices it. Breathing is part of talking. You should breathe from the midsection every few seconds, maybe every four or five seconds at first. Later, when you master correct breathing, you can vary your intake.

Q: For anyone with voice trouble, isn't it better to wait awhile to see if the problem clears itself?

A: Waiting is not the answer. Troubled voices generally do not correct themselves. Waiting will only delay the retraining process and, in far too many cases, it worsens the problem. A proven way to correct many types of voice disorders is with voice rehabilitation.

Q: A confidential voice is essential for me. As a teacher, I like to use such a voice in the classroom, and it seems to appeal to the students. But the voice does not carry, and it tires easily. What do you suggest?

A: The confidential voice is one which affords intimacy to the listener, and allows you to keep your voice down. In some places it is an effective voice. But for the classroom where there are many students to be reached, it is necessary to alter this type of voice by slightly increasing volume. To do that you must have firm control of midsection breathing. You also need to raise your pitch somewhat, because the higher pitch carries better with less effort. Your voice will then be more effective in the classroom.

Q: I frequently have a "frog" in my throat. What does that mean?

A: Many allergists feel that a frog, or phlegm, is due to allergy problems, but my experience reveals it is a wrong voice more often than not. Talking too low or too high in pitch, and deep in the lower throat, can create phlegm, along with repeated throat clearing. There is a mucus gland right under the vocal cords, and when you squeeze the gland, which happens when you talk too low or too high in pitch or focus, mucus is released to protect the vocal cords. Talking at the right pitch and tone focus takes the pressure off the lower throat, and relieves throat clearing.

Q: Why are people surprised when I tell them I am training my speaking voice? Many people train the singing voice. My job requires a lot of talking and I want a good speaking voice. What is so strange about training it?

A: Nothing. People who react to you like that think the speaking voice cannot be changed or improved. You, however, have the good sense to realize how important your voice is to your career and to protect and improve it by seeking appropriate training. Essentially, the trained speaking voice is a fulfillment of your voice potential.

Q: Once I learn to breathe correctly from my midsection, will the technique remain with me?

A: Yes, unless you completely ignore what you have been taught. Under tension, or similar states, you might forget your training, or overlook it, but you will essentially retain your correct breathing pattern, if you learned it well in the beginning.

Q: Is it really necessary to listen to the replay of my voice as I practice vocal exercises? Hearing myself makes me uncomfortable.

A: It is very important to listen to yourself in order to get acquainted with your real voice. To hear its tone, to accept it, like it — and then feel comfortable with it. At first, you don't even know your tone. The old pitch is more comfortable for you compared to the new pitch, and the old tone focus is more comfortable compared to the new one. But that is only for the present. The new tone focus and pitch range should save your voice and give you a permanent, durable, comfortable voice. It should remain clear and easy, and you can use it as you wish throughout the day.

Chapter 4

WHY YOU SOUND THE WAY YOU DO

WHY VOICES GO WRONG

Stan, a real estate salesman from the Midwest, came to see me last summer. He said he had an allergy that was affecting him both on the job and at home. He showed none of the usual signs of allergy, such as red, watery eyes and congestion, but he repeatedly cleared his throat as he talked. Stan's doctor told him that his nose was the problem, so he had surgery for a deviated septum. That, and three years of allergy shots, failed to help.

"Is it a virus?" Stan asked, clearing his throat once again.

"I think your problem is your voice," I said.

"My voice? Then why do I feel something in my lower throat, like a lump? And why do I get hoarse all the time?"

"Because you are talking incorrectly and you don't know it."

Stan had a voice that held to the bottom of his range. He was squeezing his voice out from his lower throat causing the throat clearing and hoarseness.

Another patient, Jenny, was an executive secretary. She came to me complaining about year-round sore throats, which she blamed on the ventilation system in her office: air conditioning in the summer and heat in the winter. Jenny sang in a choral group several nights a week. To protect her sore throat, Jenny's choir master told her to lower her pitch. So Jenny not only began singing but talking in a lower voice. Her throat continued to be sore and grew hoarse.

When I told Jenny that she was practicing "voice abuse," she objected. It was a negative term, she said, implying intentional harm to oneself. She much preferred the word "misuse."

Whether you call it abuse or misuse, Stan and Jenny were unknowingly causing their own symptoms and problems. Fortunately, after instruction in the Cooper voice techniques, and practice, both overcame their voice problems and developed new, stronger voices.

Whatever you call it, the fact remains that the human voice often is the most abused and misused organ in the human body. Millions of Americans suffer from laryngitis, hoarseness, throat clearing, coughing, tired, failing, and troubled voices. They don't realize that these symptoms may be caused by using the wrong voice.

Throat clearing is one of nature's most common ways of telling you something is wrong with your voice. Coughing is another. Your doctor may prescribe drugs to correct these symptoms, but are they listening to your voice?

A voice that is right may soon go wrong with too much alcohol. You become so relaxed that your voice drops down into your lower throat, the danger zone.

Laryngitis has many different causes, including smoking, the common cold, and various medical problems. When these possibilities are ruled out, the most common factors that create and prolong everyday laryngitis are vocal abuse and misuse.

If you suffer from laryngitis without medical cause, on a regular or continuing basis, you know that it does not go away easily. You have tried rest, pills, steam, gargles, shots, even vocal rest, and still it persists. Can anything be done? Yes, indeed.

You must learn to focus your voice with moderate volume. Do not try to compete with noise.

A common cold often lowers the voice pitch and brings it down to the lower throat. The tendency is for an individual to protect the voice by keeping the pitch down. Unfortunately, since that voice really isn't the natural or normal voice, the voice gets tired and hoarse, or it fails, creating laryngitis.

When a cold strikes, try to keep your "before the cold" voice going. If the pitch drops, bring it back up to your right pitch level and mask focus. The question is, how do you remember what your pitch level was before the cold started?

Use the exercises in Chapter 2 to relocate your correct pitch and tone focus. If you have any doubts use the Cooper Instant Voice Press with the "hmm-hmm-hmm" and the "ah-ah-ah."

Next time you have a cold, test your voice and your voice agility in this simple way. It should keep you talking, feeling better and doing better.

Our voices have a way of telling us when they are going wrong. Listen to the warning signals: the coughing, throat clearing, voice fatigue, and so on. If your voice sounds bad, it probably is bad and will not become better until you learn to talk correctly.

SYMPTOMS RELATED TO VOICE MISUSE

In my thirty years as a voice and speech pathologist, I have found that certain symptoms are related to the misuse and abuse of the speaking voice. I have all my patients fill out a Voice Evaluation Chart (see pages 52 and 53) which pinpoints negative sensory and auditory symptoms indicating a wrong voice. Here is a chance for you to evaluate your own voice. At the end of therapy, I have the patient fill out the form again. Also, I have my patients see a laryngologist for a laryngeal examination at the beginning of therapy, at the end of therapy, and as needed during the therapy process. The symptom chart and the laryngeal examination allow me to follow the patient's progress, along with the playback of the new voice.

HOW TO FOCUS ON YOUR NATURAL SOUND

The voice is like a camera; to work properly it has to be in focus. When the voice is out of focus, the sound is off. Ears close, minds stray. Words drop dead in mid-air.

Most voices need to be refocused. Not knowing that can result in the negative auditory and sensory symptoms noted in the Cooper Voice Evaluation Chart, shown on pages 52 and 53.

When the voice is out of focus, its energy level is sharply curtailed, so you have to push more to talk. That makes talking tiresome for you and puts a strain on your listeners. Talking should be effortless. It is one of the great pleasures of life, yet how many people can say that after talking for a time?

To find your natural sound, the voice must be focused in the mask, not in the vocal cords which produce a thin sound. People who squeeze their voice from the lower throat, wind up with troubled voices, and possibly more serious problems. When you talk with nasality these problems do not occur. You simply create "ear pollution."

It is so easy to focus your voice in the mask area by practicing the simple humming exercises, along with the Cooper Instant Voice Press. Focusing your voice may take only seconds, but learning to use your voice correctly in conversation takes time and practice. The effort will be worth it. Not only can you hear the difference between your old habitual voice and your new natural voice, you can *feel* it.

VOICE EVALUATION CHART

NAME _____ DATE _____

SENSORY SYMPTOMS   ELIMINATED

__ 1. Non-productive throat clearing   _____
__ 2. Coughing   _____
__ 3. Progressive voice fatigue following brief or
       extended voice usage   _____
__ 4. Acute or chronic irritation or pain in or about
       the larynx or pharynx   _____
__ 5. Sternum pressure and/or pain   _____
__ 6. Neck muscle cording   _____
__ 7. Swelling of veins and/or arteries in the neck   _____
__ 8. Throat stiffness   _____
__ 9. Rapid voice fatigue   _____
__ 10. A feeling of a foreign substance or a "lump" in
        throat   _____
__ 11. Ear irritation, tickling or earache   _____
__ 12. Repeated sore throats   _____
__ 13. A tickling, tearing, soreness or burning
        sensation in the throat   _____
__ 14. Scratchy or dry throat   _____
__ 15. Tenderness of anterior and/or posterior strap
        muscles   _____
__ 16. Rumble in chest   _____
__ 17. Stinging sensation in soft palate   _____
__ 18. A feeling that talking is an effort   _____
__ 19. A choking feeling   _____
__ 20. Tension and/or tightness in the throat   _____
__ 21. Chronic toothache without apparent cause   _____
__ 22. Back neck tension   _____
__ 23. Headache   _____
__ 24. Mucus formation   _____
__ 25. Arytenoid tenderness   _____
__ 26. Trachael pressure   _____
__ 27. Anterior or posterior cervical pain   _____
__ 28. Pain at base of tongue   _____

VOICE EVALUATION CHART (continued)

AUDITORY SYMPTOMS   *ELIMINATED*

___	1. Acute or chronic hoarseness	___
___	2. Reduced voice range	___
___	3. Inability to talk at will and at length in variable situations	___
___	4. Tone change from a clear voice to a breathy, raspy, squeaky, foggy, or rough voice	___
___	5. Repeated loss of voice	___
___	6. Laryngitis	___
___	7. Pitch too high; pitch too low	___
___	8. Voice too nasal; voice too throaty	___
___	9. Voice comes and goes during the day or over a period of months	___
___	10. Clear voice in morning, tired/foggy voice later in day	___
___	11. Missed speech sounds	___

YOUR NATURAL VOICE — IS IT REALLY YOU?

"I've talked like this all my life," I said, purposely exaggerating a high-pitched nasal twang. "It's hereditary. Everyone knows this is my natural voice. I just open my mouth and it comes out. Isn't that right?" I was speaking at a symposium of hospital administrators.

"I don't agree," a gentleman in the audience responded.

"Are you saying, sir, that you do more than open your mouth and talk? Do you really believe something else affects your voice?"

The man, who identified himself as Terry, paused for a moment before saying, "Your anatomical parts create the voice ... the sound."

"And the voice you are using is your real, or natural, voice?"

"I assume that's right."

I invited Terry to join me on the speaker's platform. I asked him to hold his hands above his head and say a few buzz words. Within a minutes, Terry's voice had dropped in pitch. He had found his natural voice.

"Can you hear the difference?" I asked.

Terry nodded, and smiled sheepishly.

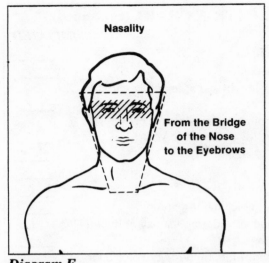

Nasality

From the Bridge
of the Nose
to the Eyebrows

Diagram F

The people in the audience could hear Terry's new voice, too — his natural voice — and they liked what they heard. His new, natural voice was better than his old one: richer, fuller, and more confident.

Terry's old voice had a definite nasal resonance. A nasal voice is generally located too high in pitch, with excessive nasal resonance. (**See Diagram F**) Saying such buzz words as "right" and "no" with your hands raised above your head often will help lower your voice tone, making it richer and fuller, while softening, if not eliminating, the offensive nasal sound. You may not hear the changes in your head, but you should on a tape recording. Once you find your natural voice level, it is up to you to retain it by practicing the simple exercises.

Whether you are talking with people in person or on the phone, in business or social relationships, the right voice can help you lead a more productive life, and a healthier one, too. My files are filled with tapes of doctors, lawyers, teachers, executives, entertainers — people from all professions — who talked with a nasal voice because they believed that the voice they were using was the only voice they had.

Not all voices are as easy to correct as Terry's. Not long ago, a desperate young man came to see me after seeking medical help across the country. He'd had different kinds of checkups and speech therapy, without success. His voice was high-pitched, almost a falsetto, and was badly strained. For 20 years, Harold had been speaking incorrectly.

Too often a doctor will look down your throat and take tests, but he may not be listening to your voice. So you go on talking as you do, complaining as you should, and getting worse.

"I can't go on like this," he told me. "Everyone makes fun of me. At times it gets so bad I want to kill myself."

I asked him to raise his hands above his head and say "no."

"No," he said in his weak voice.

"Say 'no' like you mean it."

"*No!*" His voice was lower, clearer and stronger.

"Say 'right'."

"*Right.*"

"Good. Now, lower your arms and press your 'magic button'."

"My what?"

I explained the Instant Voice Press to him, and he began humming while pushing lightly below his sternum in a staccato motion, first using "hmm," which sounds like "hmm-hmm-hmm," and then "ahhh," which sounds like "ah-ah-ah-ah."

It took about 10 seconds to find his natural voice, the voice that made him sound like a man. At first, he was shocked at the change. "I sound hoarse," he said, reverting to his old, high-pitched sound. "It's not my normal voice, the one that wants to come out."

"No, it's not your normal voice," I told him, "it's your *natural* voice."

Harold agreed to use the new voice and completed therapy. He later wrote to me that his new voice turned his life around, improving it professionally and socially.

People ask me how I know a natural voice from a normal voice. I tell them I can hear it. You can learn to hear it, too.

With a natural voice, an individual's vocal chords are clear. The properly used voice grows stronger, not weaker, as the day goes on.

The normal voice can be shrill, nasal, thin, guttural, too high-pitched or too low-pitched. "Too everything" but right. It can also be harsh and irritating, difficult to listen to, and unappreciated.

Actually, the majority of people who misuse their voices have a pathology as well. All too frequently, these people clear their throats when talking. They have trouble being heard, and their voices fade or fail. They constantly are asked to repeat themselves. And they experience neck aches and pains. These symptoms are signals of trouble ahead.

WE ALL HAVE "STAR QUALITY" VOICES

"I hate my voice," Jennifer said, darkly. "It turns people off."

"Then why not change it?" I asked.

"Oh, I couldn't do that."

"Why not?"

"Because it wouldn't be *me* anymore."

"What do you mean?

"If I didn't use *my* voice, my *real* voice, I'd sound very strange. No, worse than strange. Phony. Not like me, like somebody else."

"But you said you don't like your voice."

"I don't. No one does."

"Then do something about it. Change it."

"I can't," Jennifer said. "I don't want a new voice. I wouldn't like that either."

Jennifer wasn't the first person I had encountered who was put off by the suggestion of "a new voice." To her, like so many others, new meant artificial, unnatural. What she didn't realize was that the voice she had been using all along was artificial. She had never learned to let out the rich, beautiful voice that is within all of us.

There is so much emphasis today on being *natural*, yet so many people completely ignore their voices. They let them go unattended while they speak incorrectly, masking the God-given NATURAL sound that they could be using.

We all have potential "star quality" voices — voices that are strong, full and effective. But too few of us use what we have because we don't realize it is there. From childhood on, we ignore our voices. We use voices that misrepresent us, and detract from who we really are. In other words, *your dynamic, natural voice is not speaking for you.*

Consider the time and money you have spent (and that was spent on you) over the years to develop your mind, your body, your appearance and talents. There were new clothes, books for school, perhaps braces, glasses or contact lenses, and lessons of one kind or another. Then you talk, and ruin it all.

Isn't it time to pay attention to your voice so that it may represent you both as you are and as you want to be?

Isn't it time to start developing your natural voice?

Your voice can be your fortune, yet you squander it away by using sounds that hurt you socially, professionally, and physically, as well.

The few seconds it takes to find your natural voice are worth spending. Raise your arms above your head and say the buzz words. Press your "magic button" (the Cooper Instant Voice Press). Then follow-up with the exercises discussed earlier to develop your natural sound. You can do them without anyone realizing it. Hum the first line of a simple tune when you are alone. (Caution: do not practice "humming along" to your favorite records or songs on the radio. The humming must be in your natural key, not that of the song being played.) When you are with people, respond with "um-hmm" whenever possible. No one will be offended. In fact, such a response is appreciated. It tells them you are listening to what they are saying. And remember, when you are alone, use a brief, sharp "hmm."

Why not practice this very moment? Hum the first line of "Happy Birthday." You might even hum the words in this book as you read along.

QUESTIONS & ANSWERS

Q: Is throat clearing emotional or is it a nervous habit?

A: Repeated throat clearing is often caused by poor voice habits. Nerves may trigger it initially, but are a minor cause compared to misuse of the voice.

Q: My husband has a poor voice, which limits him in his work. He won't seek help because he believes we are born with the voice we have—either a good voice or a bad voice. Is this true?

A: No, it's nonsense. We inherit only the basics. Some of us are naturals, but the rest of us learn poor pitch and tone focus from friends, relatives and society in general. In fact, almost everyone is born with the ability to have a star-quality voice. Genetically, physiologically, and psychologically the potential is there. Don't let wrong thinking limit your husband's chances for success.

Q: Why does it take so long to recover from a voice problem? I spent almost nine months trying to regain my voice. I must admit my voice was terrible and barely audible, but why nine months?

A: Few patients are referred to rehabilitation at the first signs of a voice disorder. The problem usually has gone on for many years, resulting in a long recovery period. It takes time, effort, and specific direction to overcome serious voice problems.

Q: My girlfriend has been complaining about her voice lately. She sings in a choir, and after practice her throat aches and her voice is hoarse. Should that happen?

A: No, not if the voice is used correctly. The symptoms you describe are caused by the wrong method of singing. Her larynx and throat, and subsequently her speaking voice, are showing the effects of the misuse of the singing voice. She should see a teacher of singing for proper training, so she can learn to sing without straining her voice.

Q: I am a teenager with a really nasal voice, like I talk through my nose. I hate the way I sound. It turns people off. What can I do?

A: You don't have to sound nasal when you talk. Nasality is simply a sound created by using your voice incorrectly. You need to cut down on the excessive nasal resonance by adding *oral* resonance to your voice. The steps to do this are outlined in this chapter and Chapter 2.

Q: My voice is hoarse a good part of the day. I hardly raise it at all with the kids, but it is still hoarse. What should I do?

A: You are obviously misusing your voice pitch and tone focus. Somewhere along the line, you lost the placement of voice. It may have occurred overnight, so to speak, due to a cold or some incident, or it may have happened over a long period of time. Learn to use your natural voice. That means, learn to place your voice in the mask, where all good voices are placed.

Q: Do most patients accept that they have a voice problem that was created, and perpetuated, by voice misuse?

A: Rarely. Initially, most patients find it hard to believe that they have a voice disorder. They feel the voice is "normal," and that something else is causing the problem.

Q: Are voice difficulties universal?

A: Yes. The speaking voice often needs direction and training to develop its naturalness and beauty. There are influences everywhere which deter it from becoming a natural, attractive voice.

Chapter 5

VOICE TALK

IT'S THE VOICE THAT COUNTS

There is no avoiding the sound of a person's voice. You hear it and it influences your judgment. Something about it either attracts you or repels you.

When a voice is right, you want to hear more. When a voice is wrong, you want to cringe. That is not usually possible.

A beautiful voice can be mesmerizing. On the other hand, the most intellectual individual may be taken lightly, even ignored, if represented by a troubled or poor voice.

When Ron first came to my office he spoke very quickly, machine gun-style. His speech was clear one moment, muddled the next.

"People think I am drunk." Ron said with some clarity. He wasn't drunk, but he sounded that way. His words slurred. They came in great bursts, bunching together in unintelligible heaps.

Ron blamed his problem on an inferiority complex. Growing up, he was the youngest child in his family. When he talked, no one paid attention to him. He learned to talk fast so that he could get in everything he wanted to say.

As Ron's speech grew faster, his voice rose, along with his pitch. His voice became light and thin. He became what is known as a "mush-mouth speaker."

Ron now has a bass-baritone voice, which he found through the simple humming and "um-hmm" exercises. His new voice is his natural, true voice. It is rich, full, and strong. Ron likes his new voice, and so does everyone who hears it. People listen, and Ron can't believe his good fortune. He still rushes his words, but not as much as before, and he is learning to slow down.

Poor speech habits or patterns can lead to problem voices, and create problems for the individual. People who mumble, who talk in a monotone, whose voices are too high, too low, too thin or too nasal, generally turn off their listeners — no matter how knowledgeable they may be. Conversely, a beautiful voice can be hypnotic, even while reading the telephone book. A beautiful voice touches the head and the heart. It sells.

VOICE TYPES

The police have been using voice identification prints for years. A voice, like a fingerprint, is unique to every individual, which means that there are millions of voice sounds and combinations of sounds. However, despite all the combinations, all the variations, accents, twangs, and so on, I categorize two principle voice types: covert and overt.

Virtually everyone knows the comedy teams of George Burns and Gracie Allen, Bud Abbott and Lou Costello, Dean Martin and Jerry Lewis, and Lucille Ball and Desi Arnaz (also, Lucy and Vivian Vance, who played her sidekick, Ethel). Remember Stan Laurel and Oliver Hardy, or Jackie Gleason and Art Carney?

In every pairing, one of the members had a covert voice, while the other had an overt voice. Jackie Gleason, for example, was the overt voice — intense, outgoing, aggressive — and Art Carney, as Gleason's foil, was covert — indirect, less driven and less decisive, and rather plodding of sound.

President George Bush's voice is overt, but negative in his sound and style. Jessie Jackson is both overt and covert, depending upon time and place. Martin Luther King was overt, and stunning in his warmth and charisma.

Oprah Winfrey is overt, as are Jane Pauley and Bryant Gumbel. No question about Larry King and Morton Downey, Jr.

Dr. Ruth is covert, trying to be overt — and making it. Many show business people who have overt voices when performing may use covert voices off stage.

Many people think overt voices, being the more dynamic, would command the most attention. That isn't always the case. A covert voice can be most appealing, showing subdued strength and sensitivity. The two voice types, in their own ways, can be used to a winning advantage.

THE MONEY SOUND — A WINNING VOICE

Some voices are so different and noticeable they become winning voices for the individuals using them. I am not recommending you imitate these voices; I am simply pointing out that these voices are not only conspicuous but also extremely profitable as a calling card and trademark. Some are well-used voices; some are not. But they are all money voices, that is they make money for the persons using them.

The list of top money voices is ever changing. Inevitably, the selection must be limited to people who are highly visible. Rather, they are *audibly* visible.

Here are thirteen of the best money voices in America. Each has a distinctive sound that is worth a fortune.

1. Former President Reagan — with his voice he could replace all television news anchors. Politics aside, he continues to have the most trusted voice in America. True grit, and more.
2. Dr. Ruth Westheimer — the most unforgettable voice of our time. Once you hear her, you are never the same again.
3. Henry Kissinger — sounds like his batteries are worn down. He makes Sylvester Stallone sound great.
4. Joan Rivers — a voice ahead of her times. When she talks, E.F. Hutton listens.
5. Dennis Weaver — makes you think the Old West is alive and well.
6. Howard Cosell — the most successful escapee from a voice class.
7. Mr. Rogers — caution: for kids only.
8. Julia Child — sounds like she's wearing tight clothing that is pinching.
9. Sylvester Stallone — the greatest mumbler of our day, replacing Marlon Brando.
10. Woody Allen — he has an aura of doubt, anxiety and insecurity. A nebbish to the core.
11. Paul Harvey — super-charged voice, ideal for morning wake-up calls.
12. Telly Savalas — everybody loves ya, baby.
13. Michael Jackson, the singer — who seldom speaks in public.

Rounding out the "top 30" are: Bob Hope, Pee Wee Herman, Roseanne Barr, David Brinkley, Kirk Douglas, Clint Eastwood, Gregory Peck, Katherine Hepburn, Sandy Duncan, Tiny Tim, Roger Moore, Walter Cronkite, Don Adams, Suzanne Pleshette, Brenda Vaccaro, Bea Authur, and James Stewart.

Arthur Godfrey, one of the greatest salesmen of all time, ranks high on the list of "Hall of Fame" money voices. So do Humphrey Bogart, Walter Brennen, Ronald Colman, Bert Lahr, Margaret Hamilton, Orson Welles, Charles Boyer, Jack Benny, Henry Fonda, Rosalind Russell, John

Wayne, Peter Lorre, Rod Serling, Gary Cooper, Richard Burton, Sidney Greenstreet, Marilyn Monroe, and Cary Grant.

HOW TO BE HEARD, LISTENED TO, AND LIKED

There was a time, many years ago, when communication was either in person or by the written word. Today, people rely on voice more than ever before. It has been estimated that up to 89% of all communication is by voice.

Voices come flying at us from all directions, across dinner tables and desk tops, through loud speakers and intercoms, on radio and television. Communication has become an art, but the key to being heard, listened to, and liked is *sound*.

Some voices have a feel-good sound. They touch you; you trust them. They make you *want* to listen. Others make you cringe. You probably can name three or four of your favorite voices, and a like number of your least favorite.

It may surprise you that most of our top public speakers *learned* how to use their voices. That includes everyone from Dan Rather and Diane Sawyer to, yes, even former President Ronald Reagan.

They, like you, were born with the God-given ability to have good and great voices. But you need direction to make your true, natural voice speak for you. You have to learn whether you should talk higher or lower in pitch, how to focus your voice, and how to breathe correctly for speech.

Ronald Reagan learned to speak correctly long before he was elected to public office, and he never forgot those lessons. He has the most trusted voice in America. He is the best example of where a good voice can take you — and how it can help you stay there. His voice is his personality; he is perceived as a "nice guy." People relate to him because of his voice.

Reagan is without a doubt the greatest communicator of our time. Despite his years, his voice shows signs of aging only now and then. He may sound *tired* on occasion, but seldom old. Bob Hope, who is eight years Reagan's senior, has a voice that sounds as young and spritely as ever, without a hint of voice trouble or fatigue. That is because he learned how to speak correctly, too.

No matter what your age, if you are using your voice correctly there is no reason to lose it until you draw your last breath, barring a severe medical problem affecting the voice. In fact, there is no reason not to have a feel-good, sound-good voice that communicates who you are to the world. When you have a voice that talks for you, people pay attention.

VOICES IN THE CROWD (PARTY TALK)

It is almost inevitable that you won't come home from a cocktail party with a clear voice. It is also a good bet, depending upon how talkative you are, that your neck muscles will ache and you will have trouble speaking for the following few days.

Parties, sporting events, and other large gatherings are not only fun but great places to meet people and make deals. They are also rough on voices. That's because you talk, and keep on talking, despite the clatter of the surrounding crowd. You try to talk under the noise, over it, around it, above it—and nothing helps. You talk and you talk, and by the end of the evening, you have very little or nothing left. Your voice is either going or gone.

Most people never think about their voice when they are headed for a fun time. Even if they did, they would probably forget once the party got rolling and the refreshments started taking hold. So they talk on and on, pushing their voice, forcing it, squeezing it—losing it. By the time they feel something going wrong in their throat, it may be too late. The simplest way to deal with the problem is not to talk at all. That, of course, is impossible. The next best solution is to talk very little, which is not acceptable.

What can they, or you, do? Try this:

If you are a man with a low-pitched voice, in the bass range, talk in the upper portion of that range or switch to a low baritone, but be sure to use the mask focus. If you are a low baritone, raise your pitch and speak in a little higher range. The same holds true for women with low contralto voices. Move to a slightly higher range and remember, focus in the mask. The higher pitched voices are easier to hear and understand, easier to project, and less fatiguing on the throat and voice.

People who insist upon keeping the voice focused in the lower throat, and pitched low, are lost before they start. The noise level at public gatherings has been measured by physicists, and they tell us the din is too overpowering for the normal voice to hold its own. To be heard above crowd noise without getting a sore throat, it is wisest to speak in a higher pitch and with mask focus.

If you feel you cannot comfortably raise your pitch, or if you insist on speaking in your habitual voice because the change may harm your voice image, you have several other options. Stick close to your group and speak into the listener's ear when you have something to say. Also, stay away from the center of noisy conversations. If you are able to maneuver people, try to relocate the conversation to the fringes of the party.

You don't have to strain your voice and throat when you talk in crowds. Raise your pitch, not your volume, talk in the mask, and talk *into* (not above or below) noise; you should feel better after the hoopla is over.

QUESTIONS & ANSWERS

Q: Can "over-talking" tire the voice?

A: If you are misusing or abusing your voice, it will probably tire and give out. But, if you are using your natural voice, you'll be able to talk as much as you want or need to talk. "Over-talking" doesn't exist with a healthy, natural voice.

Q: Do many people have a monotone voice?

A: In my opinion, many people have poor voices, but not many have a true monotone voice. That is, a voice that has no variation of pitch, tone or volume. However, to the average listener, a voice that is boring, dull, lifeless, or makes little or no impression, often may be termed "monotone."

Q: My girlfriend wants me to listen to myself and find out about my voice. She says voices "type" a person. Is that true?

A: Yes, your voice is your identification. It reveals, often louder than words, if you are strong or wimpy, overt or covert, cheerful or whiny, sincere or not. The label you are given may not truly represent you or your personality, but that's the way it is. People often accept you — or reject you — by what your voice tells them, at least until they get to know you much better.

Chapter 6

THE COLORS OF VOICE

THE SOUNDS THAT REPRESENT US

The sound of your voice can affect you socially and professionally. An outgoing, strong, healthy voice is listened to and liked. A voice that is troubled, tense, distant and inaudible is a turn-off.

To hear Harry on the phone, or even in person, you would swear he is one of America's "most wanted." He sounds rough and tough, quite intimidating, but actually, he is a pussycat. Harry's friends overlook his voice, knowing it doesn't represent the real Harry. People who don't know him tend to shrink away. Harry is often offended by this reaction, but he won't be much longer. He has found his new voice — a higher-pitched, gentler voice — and he is practicing to retain it.

Another patient, Jan, used to speak in a sexy, sultry tone like Lauren Bacall. Lowering the voice to sound sensuous is quite common, but Jan talked "sexy" all the time, and it caused her problems. "I don't know why men come on so strong to me," she confided one day. "I'm not looking for anyone." Jan truly didn't realize the "vibes" she was sending out with her voice. She was unintentionally speaking in a "come hither" way.

Your voice can turn people off when you want to turn them on, and it can turn people on when you don't mean to. Everyone relates to sound. Such is the power of the voice.

You probably don't realize what you are doing with your voice, or how you are reaching out and touching people with its sound. When you first listen to yourself on tape, you may be surprised (if not shocked) at what you hear. You swear the voice on the playback is not you — or the you that you hear in your head. But it *is* you and though, like a lot of people, you don't like that other voice, you don't do anything about it. Instead of improving your voice, you go on sounding the way you always have.

Most successful people have voices that represent them as they really are. Others, whose voices are not fully effective, have learned to talk in a manner that commands respect and attention.

GAMES PEOPLE PLAY WITH THEIR VOICES

Actors may talk one way on stage, and another way in person. Doctors may have one voice for their patients and another voice at home. So may attorneys, executives, salespeople, teachers, and just about everyone who deals with the public. Nearly all "play games" with their voices. Chances are, so do you.

Have you ever noticed that you talk differently on the phone than you do when you are face to face with someone? Or that your phone voice differs from call to call? You talk one way with men and another way with women. You have a voice for friends and a voice for strangers and business associates. You have yet another voice for children and babies. A softer, gentler, more *natural* voice.

Your voice changes with the roles you assume throughout the day. In the office, you want to sound assured and assertive. At home, in a more relaxed atmosphere, you are less cautious about the way you speak.

Most people play the voice game without realizing it. Their voices change automatically, guided by mood, pressures, environment. Others play the game intentionally and so adroitly that their voices often become weapons. You've heard that voice, and may even have been a target at times. It is the voice that lashes out. It is often fierce, bombastic, and intimidating. People use that voice to make a point. The problem is, they often harm themselves physically in the process. They speak from the lower throat, pressing and straining, which not only irritates their throats but hurts their voices.

You can use different voices without pushing or hurting yourself, so long as you remember to keep the tone focus in the mask and use your natural pitch range. A different voice for different places or different people can be enjoyable, and can help make the impression you want to make.

VOICES FROM THE HEART (PET TALK)

As noted earlier, people use different voices for different situations. The voice people use to speak to pets is called "pet talk," and it truly comes from the heart.

Pet talk makes your voice warmer, more *in touch*. That is because pets humanize us. They break down our inhibitions and bring us back to ourselves, both in voice and in feelings. They allow us to behave more like we really are, if only for a little while.

"People talk" — that is, the way you talk to people — is often hard, formal, and stressful. Pet talk is endearing, easy, relaxed, and friendly.

When speaking with pets, or about pets (especially your own), another voice emerges. However, keep in mind that your pet talk voice simply reflects your ability to use different voices. It does not portray your natural voice. Imagine you have a pet with you now, and say a few words. Notice the ease in your voice, the spark, the friendliness. While the pet talk voice may not have the correct pitch or tone focus, it has a friendliness and gentleness that you may want to use in everyday conversation.

COLOR COORDINATING YOUR VOICE

When Bonnie called to set up an appointment, she didn't have to tell me what was wrong. Her voice was thin, light, airy. It was a voice without substance, one that people seldom take seriously. I tried to picture what she looked like based on her voice. A rather mousy young lady immediately came to mind.

Bonnie was young, but definitely not mousy. She was stunning to see, with a mind to match. But when she opened her mouth, the sound of her voice diminished her beauty and intelligence. "When I talk, people ignore me," Bonnie confessed. "My voice simply doesn't work for me."

Being attractive, bright, and articulate didn't help Bonnie when her voice downplayed who she really was.

"Is there hope for me?" she asked.

Not only was there hope, but she could have a voice to match her beauty, intelligence, ability, and potential. All she needed was direction. "Will you let me color coordinate your voice?" I asked.

Bonnie could not wait to get started.

She hummed, and I listened. "But I sound too loud," she said uneasily. She wasn't loud, but to her, changing from one voice to another, it seemed loud.

Bonnie's new voice was better, more effective and *different*. It was stronger, more confident, more believable, and colored with a new range of sounds and inflections. But she would have to become accustomed to it, grow to like it, until she could use it easily and naturally.

Finding and keeping your real, winning voice is like being on a diet. Unless you keep at it, it works only for a while, then you are right back where you started. If you work at reducing on a regular basis, however, your eating habits will change and, in time, the diet should show results.

The same is true for the voice.

Your new voice can represent you. It should become your trademark, your personal identification. You should not sound like anybody else. Your voice should present you at your best.

HOW TO LOSE OR SOFTEN YOUR ACCENT

Recently, an article in a major magazine reported on the rush of young urban professionals to shed their regional accents, twangs and drawls, which they feared might inhibit them socially or professionally. It is true that many people are concerned about their accents, but they are not all young. People of all ages believe that accents are stumbling blocks in their efforts to improve themselves.

Accents tend to call attention to the individual, rather than to what he or she is saying. There may be stigmas associated with accents, both domestic and foreign.

I love accents and I love New York. When I was growing up I spoke in a nasal New Yorkese, which I learned from my family and friends. Sounding like everyone else was fine as a youngster; it made me feel like I belonged. But as I got older I wanted to be more than just a sound-alike. I wanted people to notice me, the *real* me, and one of the first things I set out to improve was my voice.

As I mentioned, I love accents. They are money in the bank for some people, and an asset in many occupations. An English pub or French restaurant would lose charm and authenticity without accented waiters or waitresses. English accents add refinement and a touch of class to some establishments. Victor Borge would not be Victor Borge without his accent. How about Jackie Mason? Cyndi Lauper? Dr. Ruth? There have been hundreds of famous accents over the years. Many have been real, others exaggerated or put-on (games people play). Not all accents are endearing or attractive, however. Some work, too many others don't. Mine didn't work for me.

It was a struggle for me to lose my accent. I worked hard at it, and it took many months. That was before I discovered this simple secret: by changing the voice most accents are markedly diminished. In other words, you cannot easily retain an accent with a new voice. The key is a *new voice identity*.

The fastest, easiest way to soften an accent is to shift your voice to its natural pitch. When you change your pitch, you basically refocus your tone. The tone, believe it or not, is an essential item in creating and establishing an accent. With most people — not all — changing your voice greatly reduces the accent.

THE TELEPHONE VOICE

The host of a television talk show once asked me, "How can you tell if a voice is right or wrong, just by hearing it over the phone, without seeing the person?"

I held my hand up to his face. "How many fingers?" I asked.

"Five," he answered.

"How do you know?"

"I can see them," he responded.

"Well," I said, "when it comes to voice, I can *hear* it. That's my job."

I wasn't being flip, only honest. I listen to voices every day, and the majority of them are problem voices that can be easily corrected. Many problem voices begin with the telephone.

One client, JoAnn, is a very astute businesswoman. She runs four companies, which necessitates a lot of phone talk. "I don't know why it happens," she said, "but as soon as I start talking on the phone, my voice begins to fail. It goes hoarse in a few minutes, and I find myself straining to talk. Before I know it, I am clearing my throat."

JoAnn told me that when she talks with friends her voice is clear and easy. But when she talks business she runs into trouble.

"Why do you think that is?" I asked.

JoAnn thought for a moment. "I'm not really conscious of it, but I know I talk differently when business is involved. I'm more on guard and reserved. I'm careful what I say. With friends I seem to talk more naturally."

Many people have JoAnn's problem. On important calls, especially at work, they use a different voice, a business voice. They try to keep the volume down, and, in the process, drop the pitch and the tone focus into the lower throat. This placement causes their throats to ache and their voices to lose power. They tire easily. The more they talk, the less they feel like talking.

In today's world, talking on the telephone not only is necessary but often is the key to a successful career. Communicating by telephone need not be an ordeal. It can be fun and profitable if you use your voice correctly — keeping it up in the mask area.

Remember, practice throughout the day, a second here, a second there. In public, say "um-hmm" (people love to have you agree with them, or at least show you are listening). In private, go back to the Cooper Instant Voice Press to confirm or reinforce your correct voice placement. And, hum your thoughts, then say them aloud so you get used to the new natural voice.

WAKE UP YOUR MORNING VOICE

When you get up in the morning, your voice usually doesn't get up with you. It drags and groans. It sputters. You might refrain from talking until you have a cup of coffee or start moving around. Smart thing to do.

The morning voice can be either husky or clear. But it is often at the very bottom of the speaking range. That is because the body is essentially relaxed. There is nothing wrong with that unless you stay with that voice throughout the day. Some people do. Lots of men like the morning voice because it sounds masculine. Women often like it because it sounds sexy.

The morning voice really should not be your daily voice. It is something to lose as soon as you can, otherwise, you are talking trouble. The low-pitched morning voice can contribute to the onset and development of voice disorders.

If your morning voice is too low, it can be overcome easily by raising the pitch and tone focus as soon as you arise. If your normal voice is too high, this lower morning voice may be telling you your voice should be lower. Test it with the Cooper Instant Voice Press.

After a while, it can become automatic to correct your pitch upon rising. You need only remember to use "um-hum" to clear your voice. Then hum "Happy Birthday" or try the Cooper Instant Voice Press. Focus your voice in the mask.

THE EXECUTIVE VOICE

Motion pictures are known for stereotyping men and women executives. Typical movie bosses are usually seen (and heard) as domineering, and rather pompous, with a commanding voice. Off-screen, however, executives are seldom that way. They are simply real people with real responsibilities.

Today's executive is well-dressed, and needs a voice to match — confident, knowledgeable, alive in appearance and sound. The executive voice attracts listeners, involving them rather than turning them off. It has range and flexibility. At times it is warm and friendly, often it is firm, and generally it is dynamic, with a touch of pizazz.

The well-trained executive voice can speak in short bursts or over long stretches without tiring. It is well modulated, steady, and deceptive, for it can mask the persona behind it. It radiates self-confidence. It has authority.

Not all executive voices embody these qualities, for not all executives know how to use their voices for maximum effect. Many need to be trained in voice. They need to learn to focus their voices in the mask area, and to breathe from their midsections for proper breath control and support.

Simply put, the executive voice should be for everyone who wants to be successful.

QUESTIONS & ANSWERS

Q: My boss says I need to put some color in my voice. I've never heard the word "color" used to describe the voice. What does he really mean?

A: Without shadings, the voice is colorless. Henry Kissinger's voice has no color. It is boring. It drones. So what your boss may really be telling you, in a polite way, is that your voice isn't doing its job.

Q: I have a Midwestern accent. Some people think it is quaint and interesting, while others think it is funny that I don't do something about it. What do you think?

A: Many people are self-conscious about their accents, especially if they are relocated to another state or country. An accent, however, can be a plus, particularly in business. It can give you a distinctive sound that gets you heard, listened to, liked, and even hired. The bottom line is, if the accent doesn't bother you, or get in your way, why do anything about it?

Q: For years, I have apparently given offense by my "excited" voice. People have commented about it, and mentioned it to me in the spirit of frankness and friendliness, but I have never really understood their comments or views. That is until recently, when I actually listened to my own voice. It sounded petulant and carping. It had the tone of one given to extreme surprise that some event had taken place or that someone had done something of note. What can I do about my "excited" voice?

A: An excited tone or sound is fine for appropriate occasions, when it is real and natural. But carried over to all conditions, circumstances and events, it bores and fatigues. Now that you are aware of your problem, you can take the first step in correcting it. A lower pitch should help you speak in a more deliberate and pace manner, with less staccato volume. Also, try slowing down your rate of speech.

Q: How do you know if your voice is really representing you? I mean, showing your personality and your being?

A: You don't. People dress a certain way because it represents them. On the other hand, people use a voice because they have always used it, not because it represents them. They don't know what voice they are using, or how to use it. They simply *use a voice*. By voice training and feedback from other people, you can develop your voice and find out if you are using your voice to your best advantage.

Q: When I talk to children, why does my speaking voice go up in pitch? And, when speaking to their parents, why does it get lower?

A: Children allow you to relax and let your guard down. Parents are people you have to confront or impress, and so you may use a lower "put on" voice, if the low-pitched voice is one that you feel implies authority and strengthens your image.

Q: Do all people hear my voice the same way?

A: Your voice is heard the same way, but people don't react to it the same way. The sound of your voice is influenced by an individual's voice images, so the tone you use is received as either appealing or unappealing. People like or dislike it according to their own voice tastes and experiences.

Q: My new job requires me to get up earlier than usual. With my new, earlier hours, I have noticed that my voice is very low when I begin to talk in the morning. People tell me they like the low voice, and I appreciate the praise. I like the low voice too, but the more I use it in the morning, the less I can talk through the day. Is there some connection between my low morning voice and my lack of voice later in the day?

A: Definitely. The morning voice is, for a number of people, a very low voice. You need to raise the pitch and tone focus of your morning voice; try speaking with the voice you had before you began your new job. The low morning voice is not to be used extensively in talking. It is simply the most relaxed voice in your speaking range, the *bottom* of your voice range, and it is tiring to use too long. It fatigues your throat muscles, and tires your voice. A number of voice problems arise because people use the low morning voice. They never connect the voice problem as you did. Congratulations.

Chapter 7

TENSE AND STRESSFUL VOICES

HOW TO CONTROL YOUR VOICE UNDER STRESS

We've all heard about "big games." They come along every year in every sport, and at all levels of play: high school, college, and professional. Coaches spend long hours preparing themselves and their players so that their teams will be at their peak physically, mentally and emotionally. Motivational pep talks are part of the preparation, yet care must be taken not to go overboard.

When teams start off poorly, even the best conceived game plan can be thrown out of kilter. Sportscasters often mention, especially after early missed baskets or poorly thrown passes, that a player (if not the entire team) looks out of sync, is lacking poise and control, or is simply too charged up. A knowing "Once they settle down ...." generally follows. What it all boils down to is the jitters — tension and stress.

A team playing out of control self-destructs. It is that way with your voice, too. Your voice should sound like a finely tuned machine. Smooth, steady, strong. But use it incorrectly over a long period of time, like driving a car in the wrong gear, and it will fail.

Tension and stress due to overwork, family or money troubles, can do more than create or contribute to a voice problem. If not controlled, the problem can steadily worsen, particularly if other factors such as smoking, drinking and illness are involved. The good news is that you need not have a stress-related voice problem. You can even rescue your voice if you are in a stressful situation. Some people are simply unable to eliminate stress from their lives.

The key factor is to learn how to control your natural voice. Some people do it instinctively, others must learn.

Most people let stress go to their lower throats, and it shows in their voices through a squeezed, tired, troubled sound. Such a voice can strain your career and personal relationships. Physically, it can damage your throat and result in nodes, polyps, contact ulcers, and worse. It can also lead to a strangled voice — one that sounds like someone is throttling you as you talk.

Of course, it isn't easy to go about speaking in a relaxed way when, in reality, you are not. The secret is to be aware of your focused voice; let the sound produced from the vocal cords reach out and touch your lips and nose, and resonate there. A properly used voice should relax you, knowing that you sound strong, dynamic, confident. There is no need to relax the entire body to sound good; but knowing that you sound good should help you relax.

You can relax your voice by humming. If you are among other people, a near-silent hum or a hummed response ("um-hmm") should help you place your voice correctly.

MAKING STRESS WORK FOR YOU THROUGH YOUR VOICE

We all use adrenaline, our body's natural stimulant, to push us in our drive to be a winner. It gives us a competitive rush. But there is a downside to all that energy, especially in professional life. It used to be called "nerves." Today, it is *stress*.

Stress makes your body tense, and puts you on edge. Your voice responds by going too high or too low in pitch, often hugging the sensitive lower throat. It becomes rough and gravelly; words crack in mid-sentence. Clearing your throat doesn't help. You appear awkward and tentative. Your sound is not one of confidence.

People who are in stressful situations tend to hold their breath. It can happen at any time, no matter where you are, while driving, during an office meeting or a family dinner. Under stress your body stiffens and breathing becomes irregular, even stops for a time.

A patient with a high-pressure job recently visited my office. Speaking on the phone makes him tense, he told me. He is on the phone a lot at work, and his voice gives out. I asked him to count from one to ten. When he did, he held his breath.

"Why did you do that?" I asked.

"I don't know," he responded.

"Is that how you talk on the phone at work?"

"I guess so," he replied. "I hadn't thought about it."

I told him to have his secretary either take his calls or hold them until later in the day when he felt he could concentrate on his voice. He looked at me as if I was joking. When he discovered I wasn't, he tried my suggestion. And it worked. It worked so well, in fact, that he is now able to talk through his tension rather than suppress it.

It may work for you too. But not everyone has a secretary to run interference, or the luxury of being able to hold calls until another time.

The important point, however, is to remember to use your natural voice. To do that, you must breathe regularly and from the midsection.

Once you learn to use your voice correctly, stress can actually work *for* you, instead of against you. It doesn't matter who you are or what you do, that extra throb generated by nerves can turn a so-so voice into a winner, making it even easier to listen to — and persuasive.

Actors are probably the best example. It is a rare actor who doesn't have "butterflies" before a performance, yet they are able to step on stage, before a camera or microphone, with voices that are extra alive, rich and full. There is no better spokesman than former President Reagan. As an actor, he learned how to use his voice. As President, that voice charmed countless millions. No matter how he felt personally, he sounded relaxed, warm, and completely confident.

The lesson, then, is: Do not try to hide your nerves, use them. Let your voice speak out, not down. Speak up, but not high. Keep your voice even, and in the middle of your range. And breathe evenly. Now, you can relax, your voice is really speaking for you.

THE JOB INTERVIEW —
WHAT YOUR VOICE SAYS ABOUT YOU

Years ago, when I first started doing live radio interviews, a good friend (who also happens to be a top publicist) offered some advice. He told me: "The first 10 to 20 seconds make all the difference in the world for connecting or not connecting with your audience. Your voice will get you tuned in or tuned out." Not long after that, the book editor at a major publishing house imparted some helpful inside information. He said, "If a manuscript doesn't excite me in the first twenty pages, it is out the door."

What these two executives, both leaders in their fields, were saying was: Unless you make an immediate, positive impression, forget it.

Nowhere do these words hit home more than in a job interview. You may dress beautifully, have an impressive resume, and ooze with confidence. But the minute you open your mouth, the illusion may be shattered.

My publicist friend, who works closely with a number of prominent companies, has told me repeatedly about the importance of voice in a job interview. The voice tells all, he says, and many people are simply passed over because of their voices.

Indeed, the voice *does* tell all. It tells if you are tense, troubled, angry, distant, formal, or indifferent. It tells if you are aggressive, brash, confident, insecure, strong or weak. The view from the outside may be terrific, but your voice gives the inner you away. And the person on the other side of the desk may not like what he or she hears.

All too often, the voice makes the difference between getting hired and walking away empty handed. Few people truly realize, however, that their voices are selling them short. Most people don't want to offend, so nothing is said. It is simply "Hello" and "Thanks for coming in." And you are left to believe that you are not fully qualified (not necessarily true) or that you did not make a good impression (absolutely true).

What do *you* think your voice says about you? Do you feel it has a confident, strong, healthy sound? Or is it weak and wimpy, the type of voice even *you* feel uncomfortable being around?

There is no better time than now to find out. Say a few sentences into your tape recorder and then listen to the playback. No matter what you hear, there is almost always room for improvement. Hum the first line of "Happy Birthday" or "Row, Row, Row Your Boat," the most basic exercise, to get you started. Then say it aloud — don't sing it — as you hummed it. Follow with the "um-hmm" exercises. Feel the "buzz" that indicates your voice is placed correctly in the mask area? You should feel a tingle, a slight ring, about your lips and nose. Feel it?

Record your voice once again. Can you hear the difference between the two recordings? That is what others hear.

YOUR VOICE IS YOUR FORTUNE

You've seen how people respond to a person's voice. You know how you respond. Words are one thing, but voice is something else.

Your voice can make people like you or dislike you. It can get you hired or fired. A strong, healthy voice opens doors and creates opportunities. Your voice is a wondrous, personal identification card. And it can be your fortune if you use it correctly, naturally .

A voice that is used properly triggers a positive response. It can make friends with the people next to you, across the room or miles away — in person or on the phone. No matter what level of success you have reached, you can achieve more with a voice that commands respect and attention.

You are not stuck with a voice you don't like or one that is used improperly. If you feel you have a poor, troubled voice (your tape recorder will tell you when even your best friends won't!) then make it richer, stronger, fuller. You can, by practicing the simple exercises for only minutes a day, until your winning voice becomes habitual. How long that will take is up to you .

Once again, to locate your winning voice, hum "Happy Birthday." Remember, it is important to feel the slight balanced vibration around your nose and mouth as you hum.

Another good exercise is "um-hmm" (say it casually as if responding to a friend in conversation, with your lips closed).

Repeat these exercises from time to time each day and you should be on your way.

QUESTIONS AND ANSWERS

Q: Do nerves cause a voice problem?

A: Nerves make your body tense, and you edgy. Your voice responds by going too high, or too low in pitch, often hugging the lower throat. You may think that by talking lower you sound controlled, and that no one will know you are nervous or tense. The opposite is really true. Talking in the lower throat is a dead giveaway. But nerves can be handled in a positive way by making them work *for* you, not against you.

Nerves create the extra throb that stimulates drive and ambitions. Actors use nerves to give their voices that winning performance. Jack, an executive in your company, confides that he is tight as a bowstring. "But you don't sound it," you tell him. Jack may not believe you, but it's true. He doesn't show stress or tension through his voice. It shows up in other places. Chances are he has stomach problems or migraine headaches.

Don't try to hide your nerves. Use them to your advantage. Speak out, not down. Speak up, but not high. Keep it even and in the middle of your range. But don't let your voice be controlled by your nerves. If you ask anyone doing anything that takes effort, patience and skill, they will probably tell you they experience nerves now and then, if not often. They simply make their nerves work for them.

Q: Does a tense personality cause voice trouble?

A: Many people with voice troubles are tense, but their voice troubles are not caused by tension. They simply don't know how to use their voices. When the voice is used correctly, it sounds open, feels better, and people respond in a more positive way.

Q: What can a better voice do for you?

A: When you talk, people listen. For a little while, anyway. Your voice can turn people on or off. The sad part is, most voices don't do anything for people. They may be heard, but they probably aren't listened to, liked, or wanted.

Q: Is it true that a shot of brandy helps smooth out the voice and tone?

A: Brandy relaxes the body, and often the mind. A small amount of brandy is relaxing, but too much brandy and you have little voice control, and less voice.

Q: My voice is hoarse almost all the time. My doctor says there is nothing medically wrong, only that I am using my voice incorrectly. How is that? I have been using this voice for 45 years. Why should it get hoarse now?

A: Your doctor is right. Your voice is hoarse because you are misusing it. It happens at different ages because of different capacities to withstand vocal misuse. You must learn to use your voice properly or it will probably remain hoarse and deteriorate further, possibly causing a medical problem.

Q: How do you make a tense person less tense through the right voice?

A: People everywhere are under stress, simply because stress and tension are common in today's society. But you needn't show tension, or express it through your voice. Tension often causes the voice to rise in pitch. You can mask tension by talking in your natural range, with mask focus, rather than in the lower throat or pitching your voice too high. This makes your voice sound easy and open and friendly which makes others more relaxed with you and, in turn, you at ease with them. In addition, physical exercise can help reduce stress and tension and thereby help relax the speaking voice.

Chapter 8

PUBLIC SPEAKING: AMERICA'S SOFT SPOT

WHEN ALL EARS ARE ON YOU

You are standing alone in a spotlight at center stage, before a hushed audience that is waiting for your first words. From the moment you were asked to speak before the group, you have been filled with fear. It started with an initial rush of anxiety and continued to build.

If this brief description sounds familiar, you are not alone. Recent surveys of a wide variety of professionals — executives, politicians, and entertainers — showed 85% fear public speaking more than anything, including snakes, disease, financial disaster, even death. Which indicates that very few of us are immune to stage fright.

Despite America's fear of public speaking, more people are speaking before audiences than ever before. For some, it is a function of their executive positions; for others, it is necessary for advancement. The majority of these people have had little or no prior experience in public speaking.

Experienced or not, few people escape being nervous when in the spotlight. Everyone is concerned with what others think and feel about them. Talking in public, whether before friends or strangers, makes you vulnerable to their thoughts and feelings. Realistically, however, this is true all of your life. Public speaking simply puts you in a position where you are addressing them.

But, you say, people are staring. They aren't, really. They are *facing* you, waiting for you to tell them something. They want to hear you; they want to learn.

One of the most important factors in overcoming your fear is what I call "factor X." In simple terms, "factor X" is your personality, or rather, what happens to your personality when you step before an audience. Does it change or are you the same as in private?

Many people transform when on stage. Their personalities change dramatically. For instance, someone who is normally strong and confident may become just the opposite. Facing a crowd can do that. And that is where "factor X" comes in.

To be the best public speaker you can be, be yourself. Don't try to be forceful if you are not. Don't try to be animated or humorous or anything you are not. Be yourself.

Don't put on airs. Speak as you normally do, using words that you normally use. If you assume another personality, one that is not yours, you detract from your presentation. You won't be successful that way.

So, how can you "be yourself" when you probably have never felt less like yourself? With so many eyes zeroed in on you, your mind has gone blank, your mouth has gone dry, and your nerves are showing. One way is to let your emotions come forth. If stage fright temporarily floods you with fear, don't stiffen up and hide what you are feeling. You'll get through it. Your audience will be pulling for you; they will understand. A lot of them have had stage fright too.

OVERCOMING YOUR FEARS

Most people who speak in public, for organizations and other assorted groups, are experts in their field. They know what to say, they simply fear saying it in public. They are terrified of taking their place at the podium, of being seen and heard, but any other time they are calm and collected. The reaction is normal, especially for anyone unaccustomed to speaking before audiences.

Why the change?

An overwhelming fear brought on by insecurity. "What will people think of me?" they ask themselves. "What will they say of me? How will I come across? Can I get through it? What happens if ...?"

But when you talk in private conversation, do you ask yourself those questions? Of course you don't.

In private conversation you talk spontaneously. You may edit your thoughts before speaking at times, but you don't run scared. In public, you are scared because you are playing a role — the expert, the authority, the executive. You have something to say and you want to be sure you say it right. You can if you know your subject.

Knowing your subject thoroughly builds confidence, so it is important to do all your homework in advance. When you are familiar with your subject you can speak from a position of strength, in a less formal, more off-the-cuff manner, which is more easily understood. That is essential, especially today. Years ago, speaking in public meant giving a regimented or formal speech. Now, good public speaking is less formal. Audiences will no longer sit through long-winded oratories. Television has accustomed us to gathering information at a faster pace, and presenting it in a less stilted manner.

A major concern of every public speaker is, "What happens if ...?"

90

The worst that can happen is you forget what you've planned to say. When words fail you, don't panic. You may stand momentarily with a blank expression and an open mouth, but all is not lost. Take a breath, move about a bit, pause and recapture your train of thought. Then start over. It will help you to outline the major points you want to cover on 3" x 5" note cards. Then, if words fail, your notes can guide you along.

If talking a long time is not for you, then consider an alternate type of presentation. After a short introduction, inform your listeners that you want to know what interests them most, and that the remaining time is theirs to ask questions. Fielding questions from the audience not only takes some pressure off of you, but gets the audience involved. Audience participation is fun and generates enthusiasm. It also allows you to be more concise with what you have to say.

HOW TO SPEAK IN PUBLIC —AND LOVE IT

Most public speaking is simply giving information. Don't try to be witty. Don't be overly dramatic or serious. Serious is boring, and the cardinal sin of public speaking, or speaking anywhere, is to bore the listener. Tell what you know in a simple, direct, open way, with perspective, and then stop.

Unless you are a good actor, don't act a part when you talk in public. Be yourself. Talk naturally, as you normally would in private conversation. And don't hide behind titles. You may be someone with a long list of accomplishments, but an artificial attitude won't help your presentation. Be natural.

That isn't always easy, of course. Susan, a patient, was losing her voice when she came to me. To make matters worse, she had been asked to speak at a large meeting of company officials and employees. Susan was petrified. She was normally nervous anyway and it showed in her voice, which reacted to stress by gradually failing until she was unable to speak at all.

I tried to calm Susan by telling her to warm up before the meeting. "Practice your talk until it becomes automatic," I told her. "The president warms up. Comedians warm up. They don't go on cold; they rehearse and rehearse."

"But my bosses are tough," Susan countered. "They expect perfection."

"You don't have to be perfect to do a good job. Just know your material. Talk about it with people throughout the day. Weave portions of what you want to say into your conversations as you can. By doing so, you familiarize yourself with the material. Then give your views or position, talking naturally and directly, in a conversational manner. The people will love you."

The point is, when you talk about what you know, you talk from a position of strength. Many people speak from a position of weakness. They aren't sure of their subject, so they aren't sure of themselves. Talk from your area of strength, about what you know, and you can talk in a winning way.

Here are some added tips:

Don't stand stiffly in one spot. Stage fright can make you feel as if you are stiff all over, but you can loosen up by moving. Move your arms, your legs, your whole body. Move about freely on stage, but not excessively. Too much movement is distracting, but some movement is natural. Walk around. Shift from foot to foot. Lean on the podium, and step away from it from time to time.

Let your attention wander from one person to another in the audience. Do not stay focused on one person. Ask questions of your listeners, questions *you* would find sensible. By focusing your attention outside yourself, awareness of your stage fright should lessen — and so should the symptoms. Talk to your audience as though you were talking to someone in your home. Be friendly and giving. Show respect for them, but make your point or points.

If your voice starts shaking, walk and talk. Use hand gestures. The voice shakes because the speaker himself is shaking. By speaking up, the shakiness of the voice is overcome along with the body trembling.

Inner shaking can make you feel as if you are losing your breath. If this happens, don't try to say long sentences. Say a few words, then take a breath and continue talking. Breathing every four to five seconds throughout your talk should help overcome stage fright. Plus, it is the natural way to breathe when talking, on or off the speaker's platform.

MAKING PRIVATE CONVERSATION IN PUBLIC

With speaking in public, keep in mind that it should be the same as talking to a group of people you already know — friends, acquaintances, co-workers, or whomever. You are simply talking to a larger group than usual. It may be only slightly larger or it may be considerably more than you are used to facing, but you should talk to the audience as you do your friends. Remember, public speaking is merely a private chat made public. An exchange. Don't make it a big deal, and don't make it formal.

The more you talk in public, the more relaxed and confident you should become. To be the very best you can be, practice is essential. There is no substitute for it. You can't learn to play a piano by reading a book.

Practice speaking at every opportunity. Volunteer to speak before groups of all sizes to help diminish your fears. When speaking in public, we tend to view the audience as the enemy. They aren't. These people have come to hear you. They are on your side. Learn to be with them, to work with them, as friends.

The present emphasis on casual, conversational public speaking has made it easier than ever before. If you are wondering what approach to take, turn on your television or radio and listen. Johnny Carson, Oprah Winfrey, Phil Donahue, and others, are masters of the conversational approach.

The talk shows aren't the only programs featuring the conversational style of communication. Even the newscasters have turned from the old-style formal, "hard news" approach to the feature-style, "soft news" presentation. It is the "hit and run" method that listeners seem to like. There is a lesson here for you. Keep your talk brief and to the point.

Once again, it is essential to be fully familiar with your subject. Speak only on subjects you know. Don't bother with topics that stray from your area of expertise.

And remember, don't try to project an unnatural image when you step to the podium. You are the person the audience wants to hear, not someone else. Be yourself.

EVERYONE 'BOBBLES' BUT THEY DON'T CALL IT STUTTERING

A stutterer once told me, "If I could talk, I'd be a great success." Many others have confided similar hopes and dreams. They truly believe that the ability to talk easily will make all the difference in the world — their world.

I was never one to subscribe to that rather rosy point of view, until I ran into a gentleman who stuttered severely. When he first came to see me, he could barely make himself understood, but he did manage to say, with great effort, "If I could talk, I would make a fortune."

The man was a lawyer. But he seldom came into direct contact with the public, as most lawyers do. He worked in the back offices, out of sight and sound.

I helped him to talk smoothly again, and he made a fortune. Once he regained his speech, he moved out of the back room, where he not only faced the public but worked *with* the public.

Stutterers, like spastic dysphonics, are forever afraid of talking, fearing they won't talk well. When they try to communicate, they actually show a physiological difference from the normal individual.

If you compared the chemical and physiological makeup of an individual who stutters to that of an individual who has stage fright, I believe you would find a marked similarity. For stutterers (and spastic dysphonics) it is as if they have a perpetual case of stage fright; the pressured situation is on-going. The very thought of speaking creates stress, fear, and anxiety.

But, the stutterer lives with false images, long settled and terribly defeating. He seeks perfection of speech, an illusion that becomes the tyranny of the "I should," as in "I *should* speak perfectly." He tries to avoid the normal things we *all* do — like hemming and hawing, repeating a sound or word, mispronouncing a word, inserting vocal sighs, and using "uhs" and "ahs" — all known as "bobbles." He thinks of how he is going to talk before he talks. Worse, he thinks about the words and sounds not coming out right and it is becomes a self-defeating, self-fulfilling prophecy.

The stutterer is making himself stutter. He forces his tongue against the roof of his mouth, or tightens his lips, so that the sound can come out easily. But, by doing that, he stops the free flow of the tongue and lips, and makes the mouth a battleground for keeping in the sounds and holding back speech.

Years ago, Jane Froman was a great singing star. She was one of the most beloved singers of her day, yet few of her fans ever heard her speak. That is because she couldn't speak without stuttering. Today, we have Mel Tillis.

Mel Tillis stutters when he talks but not when he sings. Why? My explanation is Tillis breathes when singing. Singing requires breath support, as does speaking correctly. It is natural for a stutterer to forget to breathe when talking. He holds his breath, trying to talk without any air — without any breath support.

As a singer, Tillis is familiar with his material. He knows the words and feels relaxed singing them. And he knows that people like what he does. He achieved success as a singer, but as a talker? That's another matter. It is my opinion that he goes tense talking, fearing the unrehearsed words and sounds, and so he blocks and begins stuttering.

It is interesting to note that stutterers can often talk in a room alone, or talk to a cat or a dog, without stuttering. The reason is, they have no fear of judgment from others or from themselves. They are more relaxed, making it easier for them to express themselves. The breathing is relaxed and normal. Distraction also helps. Distract the stutterer from his speech by shaking his hand and, presto, he can become a normal talker. Hand shaking, or any distraction, takes the mind off speech sounds and lets nature take its course. Talking should be spontaneous, and the stutterer isn't spontaneous when talking.

Non-stutterers also often have difficulty being spontaneous and their speech is seldom perfect. Have you noticed how few people can talk without inserting "uhs" and "ums" into their conversation? And how about the thought-provoking "you know"?

Of course, it's a rare answer that isn't prefaced by "Well ... "

Well-known author and speaker William F. Buckley repeats his words and hums on sounds (carrying over his hum from one word to another), making his speech a composite of "ohs," "ahs," hums, and the other normal irregularities that constitute speech. I suggest that stutterers watch him as an example of how a normal person talks, and leave behind their dreams of perfect speech. Also, watch TV talk shows and listen to radio talk shows. Listen to how normal talkers constantly bobble when they talk. *It is okay to bobble.* Everybody bobbles. Stutterers try not to, and stutter.

Stutterers can talk and be successful. But they must get away from their ideas of perfection, which make speaking laborious and painful. Voice and speech not only should be but *can* be easy and fun.

QUESTIONS & ANSWERS

Q: How is speaking in public similar to talking in private?

A: When you talk to friends, do you ask yourself, "what if ...?" Do you think of failure? No, you say what you have to say. You are your best guide; you know the situation and the people.

When speaking in public, keep in mind that they are simply a larger group than your friends. Public speaking is merely a private chat made public. An exchange. Don't make it a big deal, and don't make it formal.

Q: I've heard some people read their speeches. They aren't Ronald Reagan. Is there another way of giving a speech?

A: There are several types of speakers: those who talk from a written script; those who *ad lib* or talk extemporaneously from notes; and those who talk impromptu or "off the cuff" without notes. I have seen those who write out their presentations and do very well. It takes a long time to do, but they have learned to do it, and they sound good.

Conversely, I like to chat from notes within my mind. I talk over the material long before I speak in public. I try it out in bits and pieces with different people in conversations everywhere, until I am familiar with the material.

The type of presentation used depends upon the speaker and the occasion. For formal and important presentations, the written approach works best. For informal and free-flowing presentations, requiring give and take, I go with the "off the cuff" style.

Q: What do you mean by being yourself when you talk in public?

A: Talk naturally. As if you are in private conversation with someone you are trying to understand and who is trying to relate to you. Don't be phony; don't be formal or different from the way you normally are. Don't look for big words, or perfect ways to express yourself. Tension comes from trying to be someone you aren't, trying to impress, or trying to be perfect. Just be natural.

Chapter 9

THE POWER OF A WINNING VOICE

THE DECLINE AND FALL
OF THE AMERICAN VOICE

Greta Garbo, Ingrid Bergman, John Wayne and Joan Crawford are but a few of the names that come to mind when recalling great movie stars of the past. "They had faces then," say longtime movie fans. The fact is, they had *voices*, too.

Lauren Bacall is known not only for her sexy, sultry looks, but for an unmistakable voice that perfectly complements her appearance. Most of us believed that she was talking naturally with her husky, throaty voice. Today, I know better.

During the Golden Age of movies, the studios often tried to alter the voices of their stars. Lauren Bacall did not have her trademark sound when she first went to Hollywood. She explained in her autobiography, *By Myself,* that her voice was low, but that it tended to rise when she became nervous or emotional. Howard Hawks, her producer/director, didn't like what he heard. "Nothing is more unattractive than screeching," he told her. He insisted that she train her voice so that it would remain low at all times.

On her own, Lauren Bacall drove into the nearby mountains, where she read aloud from a book "in a voice lower and louder than normal." She changed her voice, but she ultimately developed problems with it.

These days, people everywhere are abusing their voices by forcing an unnatural sound. They may know what they want in a voice, but they don't know how to get it.

Joan Rivers came to me when she developed problems with her voice. So did Anne Bancroft, Kirk Douglas, Diahann Carroll, and Richard Crenna—stars who rely on their voices for their livelihood. O. J. Simpson said, "After just an hour with Dr. Cooper, I noticed a change in my voice, and I had a direction to go in."

Everyone wants to be a winner. For some, that might mean speaking in a masculine way or in a sexy way; others are after a voice that rings with authority and confidence. They not only want to sound impressive, they want to make a sound impression.

Confidence, authority, leadership, and desirability are just a few sought-after qualities that form images in our minds. Those images are often transferred to the voice, making us speak as we think a person should to achieve those qualities. Without proper guidance, however, the sound becomes forced and unnatural, resulting in damage to the vocal cords.

Gershon M. Lesser, M.D., a highly respected internist in Los Angeles, believes the voice is a "second face," representing us through speech and sound. As a diagnostician, Dr. Lesser finds three-fourths of his patients complaining of sinusitis, post-nasal drip and allergy, really have voice problems but don't know it. They experience tired voice, morning voice, a failing or troubled sound, laryngitis, hoarseness, and so on. "Their problems stem from speaking incorrectly," states Dr. Lesser.

Dr. Lesser experienced a voice problem while the host of a weekly radio show, "The Health Connection." Faced with the options of surgery or voice rehabilitation, Dr. Lesser chose voice rehabilitation. I had the opportunity to work with Dr. Lesser and helped him regain his voice. His theory is, "You can always *do* surgery, but you can't *undo* it." Dr. Lesser is a leading advocate of self-help methods. His concluding comment was: "Before you think of surgery, think of Dr. Cooper's 'magic' cure; it even astounds the doctors."

The sound revolution has played a major role in the decline and fall of the American voice. We know we don't sound good, or at least as we'd like to sound, and so we squeeze and mash our voices. As a result, our voices tire and fail, become hoarse, or give us trouble by fading in and out. We clear our throats and cough. We look for a remedy to cure "outside influences." All too often, the problems are self-inflicted.

Talking can be fun and exciting, but not with a voice that is misused.

TROUBLED AND PROBLEM VOICES

When I was a guest on the TV show, *Hour Magazine*, Gary Collins asked his studio audience if anyone had trouble with his/her voice. (Collins had told me before we went on the air he did not believe very many people had troubled voices.) To his surprise, quite a few hands were raised.

100

The number was actually low since many people have voice problems without realizing it. The majority of the people who complain about sinusitis, allergies, and post-nasal drip have troubled or problem voices; yet they fail to hear what their voices are saying about them. A troubled voice says you are down when you are up, angry when you are calm, blah when you are raring to go. A troubled voice says so much. It is talking *for* you, and yet it isn't. It is talking *to* you, but you can't hear it.

Every day, we hear troubled and problem voices resulting from voice misuse and abuse. They sound erratic and strange; the voices come and go. Among the most common types of troubled or problem voices are: nasal voices, depressed or angry voices and, especially, tired voices.

You can have a tired voice at any age, but it occurs more and more as a person grows older. With lowered pitch (which also denotes despair, resignation, hostility) and poor breathing habits, the voice begins to falter and, at times, fails. The tone wavers and the volume decreases, affecting the carrying power. A person with a tired voice is frequently asked, "What did you say?"

Most cases of voice tiredness are either ignored or merely acknowledged by physicians, who have little awareness that voice fatigue is but a symptom of voice misuse. Few referrals are made to voice therapists.

The seductive voice (or bedroom voice) is often attractive, and has become the trademark of numerous celebrities. Marilyn Monroe used it. So did Jayne Mansfield, Hedy Lamarr, Lauren Bacall, and Charles Boyer. To achieve a seductive voice, you simply drop the pitch and use little volume. The word "breathy" is often associated with it.

The seductive voice is not a voice to use constantly. Use it to make a point, then return to your natural voice. The seductive voice is highly effective for specific occasions, primarily because of its confidential and intimate tone, but a lowered voice with reduced volume will irritate the vocal folds and create voice problems if used over a long period of time.

The most devastating of the voice disorders is spastic dysphonia — the strangled voice trapped in silence.

I liken spastic dysphonia to constant stage fright. Everyone knows what far-reaching effects stage fright has on a speaker. That's because there is a chemical and neurophysiological change affecting the adrenaline flow of the body when an individual talks in public, as compared to private conversation. Spastic dysphonics, I find, have perennial stage fright. They are forever afraid of talking, fearing that they cannot talk well.

Many doctors find spastic dysphonia to be an irreversible neurological problem. I believe spastic dysphonia is a mechanical voice problem. The individual with the condition is talking with the brakes on. Not realizing what they are doing, the problem continues.

Contrary to the prevailing opinion, spastic dysphonia, or what I call "the monster voice," isn't hopeless at all. It has an excellent prognosis in most cases, with intensive therapy in my office. I differ with my colleagues and medical associates in treating spastic dysphonia, as well as other voice problems. But the successful results — and the recovered patients — speak for themselves.

The late Henry Fonda came to me complaining about his strangled voice. Through my program of direct voice rehabilitation, he was able to recover his voice and go on to film *On Golden Pond*. He received an Academy Award for his role.

Andrew Simmons, a top administrator at a major West coast university, experienced voice problems dating back to 1972. He was diagnosed at a university hospital speech clinic as having spastic dysphonia, probably incurable, and discharged after being told they had done everything they could for him. It took Andrew a year to catch on to my techniques and another two years to work them into everyday speech. Today, talking properly is an automatic response. "If I find myself starting to slip back into the lower throat, I hop back up," says Andrew. And the spasticity has not returned.

Elizabeth Darling was in her 28th year as an elementary school teacher when she was told she would have to quit teaching permanently because of spastic dysphonia. She couldn't answer the telephone, let alone teach a class. She couldn't talk. Spastic dysphonia can stop careers.

Elizabeth underwent two to three hours of intensive individual therapy every weekday, plus group therapy on Saturdays. As she improved, her sessions became less intense, but she continued on a daily basis. Today, Elizabeth is back teaching with a normal voice.

A minister from the Midwest, who had spastic dysphonia for nine years, tried all kinds of therapy for his voice problem, even going to the Mayo Clinic, to no avail. A parishioner of his church gave him a copy of my book, *Change Your Voice, Change Your Life* (Macmillan,1984; Harper & Row, 1985), and he decided to seek my help. He stayed one month, undergoing intensive daily voice therapy. He recovered his speaking voice, which he calls a miracle. He phones or writes periodically to report that his voice remains fully recovered.

Henry Fonda, Andrew Simmons, Elizabeth Darling, the minister, and others, whose conditions were diagnosed as irreversible, have proven that "miracle cures" can happen.

Another serious voice problem is vocal cord paralysis. Recovering from surgery to remove a malignant tumor from the thyroid gland, Jason Chase found his voice was hoarse, lacked carrying power, and faded or failed within a few minutes of conversation. Rather than have a teflon injection into the paralyzed vocal cord, Jason, a doctor himself, elected to try direct voice rehabilitation. His surgeon, William Longmire, M.D., UCLA Medical Center, referred Jason to me. I realized, from what Jason told me, he had been having voice trouble before his surgery without knowing it. His voice had been failing and fading, but he assumed this was normal. I concluded it would take a year for him to regain his voice — a better voice than he had ever had. That was twenty years ago. Recently, Jason was on my television show, speaking with the excellent voice he worked for and obtained, under my direction, many years ago. He said he never gets hoarse or loses his voice anymore. Jason's voice is clear and efficient, yet he still has a paralyzed vocal cord. Not too long ago, I was a guest of Jason's at his hospital. Some in the medical community there found it hard to believe that Jason had ever had a voice problem. But Jason and I both knew, since we had recordings of his old voice, that once upon a time Jason had had a very serious voice problem.

A college professor came to see me, without much hope. Frank Hadley had been told that he would never have a normal voice again because of vocal cord paralysis following back surgery. In one year of voice rehabilitation, with Frank flying in to see me every other weekend, he recovered his full, normal voice.

103

In 1970, I published the results of my direct voice rehabilitation with paralytic dysphonic patients. Of the 18 patients with a paralyzed vocal cord, 14 were discharged with excellent results, fully recovered, and four with good results, being judged to be 90% recovered. Time spent in therapy for these 18 patients was 6 to 18 months. Since that time my success with this condition has continued to be excellent.

The so-called hopeless or impossible voice disorders are not that at all. Their prognosis for having normal and effective voices again is usually excellent; properly directed in my office, these people are able to successfully resume their careers and lives. No one should ever live with a voice problem when help is available. I have been called the "miracle voice doctor" by some of my patients. It has been my pleasure to be of assistance to them in recovering from what many have been told are hopeless voice problems. Spastic dysphonia, paralytic dysphonia, and growths on the vocal cords should not be treated by self-help. These are very serious voice disorders, and they require professional direction.

VOICE SUICIDE: AN OCCUPATIONAL HAZARD

Joan Rivers asks, "Can we talk?"

I say "No!" America is committing voice suicide, but no one knows it.

What is voice suicide? It's the All-American game, our newest national pastime. I find 50% of the voices around us are too thin, high pitched, nasal, causing sound pollution. At least 25% are too low and gutteral, causing voice suicide or voice burnout.

People everywhere are afflicted with it. You see and hear them every day; they are in the office, on the street, probably even in your own home. You could be one of them.

When you "push" your voice, perhaps to be heard over noise or to give directions to someone, does your voice drop so deep that your throat starts to hurt? Do you get laryngitis after a few hours of speaking in "authoritative" tones? Does your throat tighten after speaking at office meetings or in front of large groups? Is your throat "tender" after yelling at the kids all day—or rooting for your favorite sports team? These problems, and others, come from committing voice burnout.

Too many Americans commit voice suicide by misusing or abusing their voices. They talk too high and thin, too nasal; or too guttural, and too deep in the throat. They have the symptoms of voice trouble, such as throat clearing, frequent laryngitis, hoarseness, or a voice that tires. Their necks ache after talking; speaking is an effort for them. Since the voice fades, they can talk only for limited periods, and then, not as well as they might like. They find it difficult to be heard or listened to.

Misusing your voice can lead to irritation of the vocal folds or cords, even to nodes, polyps, and contact ulcers. If the misuse is persistent or extensive, it may result in a premalignancy of the cords, such as papillomatosis or leukoplakia, and, finally, to cancer of the vocal cords. Impaired voices, such as the strangled (or monster) voice can, and often do, develop from use of the wrong voice.

Voice health is an essential issue with most entertainers. For people not in show business, it is another matter. These people know they need help but they don't know what to do or where to go, and they may be hesitant to spend money to correct the problem. There also is the prevailing myth that we are born with the voice we use, and that's it. The fact is most voices can be adjusted quickly and simply in a way that is completely natural and direct.

THEY'RE NOT LISTENING

Amy was told by four physicians and three speech therapists that her voice was all but gone. When she asked the physicians what to do, she was advised to wait. Amy waited and her voice didn't come back. The speech therapists had other suggestions, but nothing worked. One by one they told her, "Your voice isn't going to come back."

What I am saying is: many medical professionals do not know how to listen to the voice. They presume that what ails the patient has to be seen, not heard.

An allergist may treat a patient who has a simple voice disorder under the mistaken assumption, or presumption, that the voice is failing or has failed because of an allergy, when no such relationship prevails. An allergy may exist, but it minimally affects the speaking voice and its efficiency. (It may affect the quality but not the basic efficiency.)

When a speaking voice fails, or is failing, many in the medical professional presume the problem is neurological or organic. If they can't find a medical cause, one they can see, they fault the patient. The problem is considered to be psychosomatic, emotional or psychological. When the patient tries the psychiatric approach, and nothing is found wanting, the patient is again faulted. The psychologist or psychiatrist also believes that the problem lies with the patient, not the diagnosis, which is presumed to be accurate. In most cases, the patient is not the failure. It is the diagnosis that sends the patient in the wrong direction.

Direction is the key to recovery. Appropriate mechanical direction — a lower pitch, a higher pitch, a different tone, a change in resonance, better breathing support — is *the* factor that enables the voice to recover.

Unfortunately, I have often found the direction given a patient is not only inadequate, but lacking completion. In time, the patient is told his case or condition is hopeless or impossible — especially when categorized as spastic dysphonia, geriatric voice or a paralyzed vocal cord. It is only the direction that is hopeless. For the patients, there is hope for 99% of the cases I see.

Too often, the simple, corrective techniques are overlooked in favor of more complicated and bizarre methods, including so-called voodoo therapy. One patient was told by his physician to chew on a golf ball for his strangled voice. Another was told to change his liquor from scotch to bourbon, and when that didn't help, to have surgery.

All too often speech therapists are not listening either. In my opinion, that is because they are not always well-trained in voice. Some simply do not know what direction to give patients with wrong or problem voices. There are documented cases of other experimental therapeutic techniques, such as working out in a darkened room, screeching like a donkey, endless hours of reading aloud from a book, and muscle crunching workouts. Still another was told to lift a chair high above his head.

Voice improvement in a patient demands competency on the part of the physicians and voice therapists, as well as cooperation from patients. These two factors, competency and cooperation, make the voice recovery work.

SURGERY: THE GREAT AMERICAN PASTIME

One woman patient had surgery for spastic dysphonia. The surgery was successful, but it didn't help her talk. She had a second operation and it too was a success, but she still was unable to talk. A nervous breakdown followed. She was recovering from that when her doctor advised her to have surgery again.

Another patient, also a woman, had been working with a speech therapist for three years. The therapist told her to read aloud from a book to correct her strangled voice. She was not told to raise or lower her pitch, how to focus her voice in the mask or how to breath correctly, only to read aloud. When that didn't work, she had surgery. She was able to speak, but only in a breathy way because the surgeon had cut her laryngeal nerve, which paralyzed a vocal cord. Six months after that, she had returned to her old spastic sound again.

Having surgery often just scratches the surface of the problem, because the real cause—a troubled or failing voice—has been left untreated. The problem generally returns, and once more surgery is recommended. The patient cannot be blamed for following the doctor's advice. We live in a "now" society. People want an immediate cure, and surgery is immediate. Essentially, surgery doesn't change a misused or abused voice. It may remove the tissue that formed on the vocal cords from using the wrong voice, but the patient ultimately needs to learn a new voice.

I have been fortunate, over the years, to be associated with the following small, sophisticated group of ear, nose, and throat doctors who refer patients for direct voice rehabilitation instead of surgery or following surgery: Robert Adair, M.D., Donald Doyle, M.D., Robert Feder, M.D., Ed Kantor, M.D., Harvey Paley, M.D., Lawrence Pleet, M.D., Joel Pressman, M.D., Monte Purcelli, M.D., Alvin Reiter, M.D., Ronald Roth, M.D., Henry J. Rubin, M.D., Joel Shulman, M.D., Sherman Strand, M.D., and Hans von Leden, M.D.

Other knowledgeable physicians that I have been privileged to work with in the treatment of voice and speech problems include: Benjamin Kagen, M.D., Gershon Lesser, M.D., William Longmire, M.D., Robert Rand, M.D., and David Rubin, M.D.

QUESTIONS & ANSWERS

Q: Can voice affect a person's physical and mental health?

A: Yes, voice has a definite affect on physical and mental health, for it influences not only careers but personal relationships. The properly used voice has a "feel good" sound. It builds confidence and makes a positive impression on others. A natural, healthy voice can turn lives around.

Q: My three-year-old son is hard of hearing and his speech is poor. Friends and associates have suggested that I wait until he is four or five for help with his speech, believing that he might outgrow the problem, at least partially. I am fearful that I might be wasting valuable time, and hurting his chances for progress. What is your suggestion?

A: For a child with a hearing handicap speech therapy, as well as auditory training, is not only appropriate but essential. There is a "speech readiness" period for a child. That is the time when the child develops his speech most fully, and most naturally. The hearing-handicapped child is deprived (to varying degrees) of the natural and normal sound stimulation that hearing children have. Therefore, the hearing-handicapped child falls behind in speech ability and development. If you wait until he is four or five, you are allowing time to waste away, and the speech readiness period to dissipate. Your son may outgrow some of his speech problem, but it is not likely, especially with a hearing problem. He needs sound stimulation and speech therapy now.

Q: My voice is often tired. No one believes me. They say it is in my mind. I keep telling them it is in my throat. Who is right?

A: You are. Misuse of the voice by incorrect pitch, improper tone focus and poor breath support results in a "tired voice." The throat aches and many allied symptoms may result. The reason no one believes you when you say your voice tires is because most people are unaware of the speaking voice and the symptoms of vocal misuse. From time to time your voice may become tired from fatigue or lack of sleep, but if you use your voice well it should remain clear and easy.

Q: My doctor tells me I have a growth on my vocal cord called "leukoplakia." He advises surgery, but I don't want surgery. What do you advise?

A: Vocal misuse, I find, can contribute to the onset and development of the kind of growth you have. Smoking is the essential cause of leukoplakia, but I have found once a person changes to his correct pitch, improves his tone focus, and begins breathing correctly, the growth can disappear. And if you do smoke, stop.

Q: How can you tell when a voice is going wrong?

A: By the symptoms. You get hoarse, your voice doesn't hold up throughout the day, your voice fades (people continually ask you to repeat yourself), your throat aches, or you find you have to push your voice. If you have any of these symptoms, then you are committing voice suicide. And you didn't even know it.

Q: I was told I have two growths called "polyps" on my vocal cords. My doctor suggested an inhaler. I tried one and it didn't work. I then tried pills, shots, gargles, vocal rest, and even bed rest. Now, because all these things failed, I have been advised to change my job. I am a salesman and I love my work. What do you recommend?

A: Polyps are benign growths on the vocal cords. Surgery can remove polyps, but since voice misuse — the wrong pitch, quality, volume, and placement of the voice — often creates them, it is essential you learn how to use your speaking voice. These growths have responded extremely well to voice therapy. But if you choose not to learn correct voice usage, you will most likely continue to experience voice difficulty. My advice is: Do not change your job. Change the way you are using your voice.

Q: I have been advised to seek voice therapy following the surgical removal of two small nodules on my vocal cords. Why doesn't the surgery take care of the problem?

A: Surgery removes only the immediate problem. The real problem that caused the nodules was voice misuse and abuse. If you don't want a possible return of the nodules, you need to learn to use your voice properly. Without voice therapy (and you have probably considered ignoring it), you might find yourself in need of the same surgical procedure again. Direct voice rehabilitation requires a voice doctor who is knowledgeable and sophisticated, to determine correct voice therapy for the patient.

Q: Can a person who is severely hard of hearing have a normal voice?

A: A patient of mine from England told me that three almost deaf boys in her family all have normal voices. They were taught voice as well as speech from early childhood by the school system. In my office, using the Voice Mirror Machine and the hum technique, individuals who are severely hard of hearing can be helped to have normal voices.

Chapter 10

THE POWER OF A WINNING VOICE

THE VOICE OF SUCCESS

Not long ago, a young man looked me in the eyes and said, "I want the voice of success."

He was a salesman, and a good one, but he wanted to be even better. He wanted to be the best. It wasn't that his voice was poor. All it needed was fine tuning to give him a competitive edge.

"If my voice doesn't give the impression that I know what I'm talking about, my clients write me off immediately," he said. "I am on the phone constantly, so it is important that people *hear* what I have to say. My voice is my future. Without a voice that projects confidence and success, I'll never be the person I want to be. And *can* be."

The young man wasn't being boastful or dramatic. He simply knew what he wanted for his life. And there are millions more just like him. Everyone wants to be a winner. Not just now and then, but all the time. It's the American Dream.

Your voice has the power to make you a winner. It can make sure you are heard, listened to, and liked. It can gain you respect, get you a job, a husband or a wife. The right voice can make you admired and help you win friends. A wrong voice, on the other hand, can cause you to be misunderstood, rejected, even fired. It can close doors. The most correct and elegant language loses all its beauty with a bad or ill-trained voice.

No matter what level of success you have reached, professionally or personally, you can achieve more with a voice that commands respect and attention.

If you haven't been a winner, ask yourself *why not*?

Is your voice holding you back? Does it trouble you when you hear yourself? Do you feel insecure when you speak? Does your voice fade and give out? Does it prevent you from being who you are, or who you want to be?

If you feel good about your voice — and, equally important, it feels good when you use it — don't bother trying to make it better. But if you feel uncomfortable, you are speaking with the wrong voice.

SUMMING UP THE SECRETS OF VOICE

Talk in the mask, the area about your lips and nose, where all voices should come from. The mask brings out the subliminal hypnotic sound that makes the voice so likeable and easy to listen to. All great voices have that sound placement and tone.

Use the buzz words to bring your voice forward. Practice your new voice as you read a book or newspaper. Say "um-hmm" as you respond in conversation. If your voice is too soft, increase your volume without forcing it. And be sure to monitor your daily progress on a tape recorder.

Breathe right, speak right. Breathe easy, from the stomach not the chest, please. Belly breathing is the way to go. Talking on air is like riding on tires with air, comfortable and comforting. As you talk, feel your stomach move in progressively, gradually, and smoothly.

How is your phone voice? Most of us have different voices for different occasions. We are voice schizophrenics, but never fear. It is normal and natural. The phone gets us to change our voices. We talk too loud or too soft, and often too low. Talk naturally. Be yourself. Don't talk in the lower throat, and don't go too loud.

If people think you aren't loud enough, or they frequently ask you to repeat yourself, speak up by pretending the other person is a little hard of hearing. People with soft voices have the ability to project. But too often, they let their voices sink down in the lower throat rather than project from the mask.

Shape up your voice quickly. You can get a voice tune up in seconds. Humming is a simple and direct way to help you find and use your natural voice — the voice that gets you heard, listened to, and liked.

Press your magic button (the Cooper Instant Voice Press). Raise your hands above your head and say the buzz words. Hum the first line of "Happy Birthday" or "Row, Row, Row Your Boat." Those exercises could not be more basic, yet they should help you find your natural voice, and relocate it whenever you are in doubt. Practice for seconds at a time throughout the day, until your new voice becomes second nature to you.

Try your natural, true voice on for size. Henry Fonda did it. Anne Bancroft, Dennis Weaver, Joan Rivers, and Cheryl Ladd did it. So did Cathy, Larry, Tom and Tobi. These people, and many others, have discovered their natural voices, and how to apply them to enhance their careers, and ultimately, their lives.

Within each of us exists a "star quality" voice. Follow the simple plan described on these pages and you should find yours. Once you do, you can be on your way to *Winning With Your Voice*. Remember, I can help you find your natural voice, but you are the person that makes the rest happen. It is all up to you.